CATHEDRALS & ABBEYS
OF ENGLAND

TEXT BY

THE VERY REVEREND STEPHEN PLATTEN,
DEAN OF NORWICH

This edition © Jarrold Publishing 1999, latest reprint 2004.

The author acknowledges the help of all the cathedrals and abbeys included in this book in taking their time to check the text for architectural and historical accuracy. The author accepts responsibility for any inaccuracies still remaining.

Text © Stephen Platten 1999.

Photographs © Jarrold Publishing except as follows: **Cover** *top left* photography Jarrold Publishing, reproduced by kind permission of the Dean and Chapter of Westminster. **Page 6** *middle* reproduced by kind permission of the Dean and Chapter of Salisbury; *bottom left* photography Jarrold Publishing, reproduced by kind permission of the Dean and Canons of St George's Chapel, Windsor. **Page 10** David Tarn Photography. **Page 11** *top and bottom* reproduced by kind permission of the Dean and Chapter of Durham. **Page 19** *top* reproduced by kind permission of the Dean and Chapter of York: *photographer* Jim Kershaw; *bottom* reproduced by kind permission of the Dean and Chapter of York: *photographer* Newbury Smith Photography. **Page 34** *top* reproduced by kind permission of the Bishop of Brentwood: *photographer* Nick Carter. **Page 41** *top* reproduced by kind permission of the Dean and Chapter of Worcester: *photographer* Chris Guy. **Page 42** *bottom* photography Jarrold Publishing, reproduced by kind permission of the Dean and Chapter of Hereford. **Page 46** *bottom* reproduced by kind permission of Dorchester Abbey: *photographer* Frank Blackwell. **Page 54** photography Jarrold Publishing, reproduced by kind permission of the Dean and Chapter of Westminster. **Page 55** *top* reproduced by kind permission of the Dean and Chapter of Westminster; *bottom* photography Jarrold Publishing, reproduced by kind permission of the Dean and Chapter of Westminster. **Page 57** *top and bottom left* reproduced by kind permission of the The Friars, Aylesford. **Page 65** *top* reproduced by kind permission of the Dean and Chapter of Winchester: *photographer* John Hardacre. **Page 71** *bottom* reproduced by kind permission of the Dean and Chapter of Salisbury.

Published by Jarrold Publishing, Healey House, Dene Road, Andover, Hampshire, SP10 2AA, UK.

Pitkin Guides is an imprint of Jarrold Publishing, Norwich.

Printed and bound in Hong Kong.

ISBN 0-7117-1003-1   2/04

Front cover pictures *clockwise from top left*: Westminster Abbey; interior view of dome, St Paul's Cathedral; exterior view of St Paul's Cathedral; Lincoln Cathedral; the view towards the Trinity Chapel, Canterbury Cathedral; Norwich Cathedral.

Inside front cover: Salisbury Cathedral.

Back cover pictures *clockwise from top left*: Hereford Cathedral; Salisbury Cathedral; Buckfast Abbey; Ely Cathedral; St Albans Cathedral; Christ Church Cathedral, Oxford; Tewkesbury Abbey; Bath Abbey; Malmesbury Abbey; Winchester Cathedral; York Minster.

Inside back cover: Gloucester Cathedral.

CONTENTS

INTRODUCTION

Maps of mediaeval England pinpointing the sites of monasteries and convents, either surviving or now long lost, are often a cause of wonder. The sheer number and distribution of religious houses, both in centres of population and in remote places, is in itself surprising. Recognition of this partially lost world indicates both the power and the influence of religious orders in the making of European civilisation. The roots of this tradition, however, go back well beyond the period of European self-consciousness and even beyond the roots of Christianity. When the Dead Sea Scrolls were discovered in the late 1940s, nearby was also discovered a second-century Jewish monastery-like complex indicating that a corporate religious lifestyle extended back beyond the beginnings of Christianity.

EARLY CHRISTIAN COMMUNITIES

In the fourth century St Antony in Egypt and St Jerome in the Judaean desert began to pioneer a form of solitary monasticism that survives in Egypt and Ethiopia until the present day. Monks lived secluded lives in separate cells that were constructed around a central church. They would come together for common worship. A similar style of religious life existed in those places where Celtic Christian discipleship was the main instrument of mission. In the rural and remote areas of Ireland, and then later in Iona and in Cornwall, solitaries would build cells around a simple church. They would use these centres as bases for missionary forays into the surrounding countryside. In the seventh century, Aidan was sent down from Iona to Lindisfarne to act as a missionary to Northumbria; he again established a Celtic-style monastery as his base. There were similar religious centres in Wales, and even one in East Anglia.

Also in the early seventh century, Augustine established his missionary centre in Canterbury, and then later his disciples moved on to Rochester. Augustine had been sent to England by Pope Gregory the Great who was himself a monk. By this time the influence of St Benedict, who had died in the mid-sixth century, was already beginning to make its mark. Benedict, who was an Italian, is seen as the father of Western monasticism. It was he more than anyone else who began to give shape and stability to that form of monasticism which was lived in community. His rule is a remarkable balance of a guideline for wholesome living and a challenge to live the Christian life. The pattern of life that issued from the Benedictine way was to become formalised in the structure of the monastery itself. It is this which helps us to understand the English abbeys and priories that have survived either completely or as ruins.

THE MONASTIC TRADITION

At the heart of the religious life stands the discipline of prayer and so the monastic church dominates in each abbey or priory. In the choir[1] the monks would gather for prayer at least seven times in every twenty-four hours; they would even rise during the middle of the night to pray. Beyond the space known as the choir, which was normally at the heart of the church, to the east would be the high altar around which the monks or sisters would gather for mass. To the west of the choir, generally beyond a wooden or stone screen, was the nave, or people's church, where mass would be sung with and for the local population, and possibly also with pilgrims. The monks would generally live in dormitories (dorters) and they would eat corporately in large hall-like refectories. There would be a guest house for pilgrims and travellers, and often a hostry (a pilgrims' hall) where travellers would be welcomed. These monastic buildings, which would also include a chapter house for conventual meetings and a library, would be ranged around a cloister. The cloister was thus the nexus of all routes, the crossroads of the

Iona Abbey, rebuilt in the twentieth century on the site of a Celtic, later Benedictine, monastery

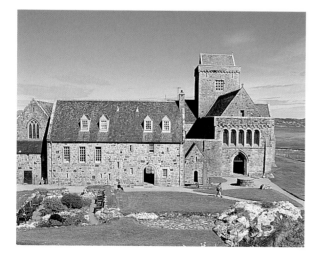

[1]The variant spelling *quire* is also used in this book in accordance with the wishes of the individual cathedrals concerned

than any other group of people for the foundation and self-understanding of mediaeval Europe. The culture of learning and the importance of the leadership of the abbot was seminal in the growth of European civilisation.

Still other religious orders developed. The mendicant (those forbidden to own property) orders of friars – the Franciscans or Greyfriars and the Dominicans or Blackfriars – were founded at the start of the thirteenth century. These orders were missionary and so were mobile in contrast to the Benedictines. Groups of secular and Augustinian canons also came to live in community. Different again were the Carthusians; the 'charter houses' in which they lived bore some similarities to early monasticism. The monks lived in separate houses and came together only for community worship; Mount Grace Priory in Yorkshire is a fine example of this expression of the religious life.

monastery. It stood at the heart of a stable contemplative community – the Benedictine rule includes a vow of stability. The monks were encouraged to stay within the bounds of the monastery and not to be wanderers; Benedict has harsh words to say about peripatetic monks.

As the Middle Ages progressed, so other orders developed. In the twelfth century a stricter interpretation of the Benedictine vows, pioneered at Citeaux in southern France, gave birth to the Cistercian order. The asceticism here was harsher and the geographical position of the monasteries generally remote – Fountains and Rievaulx Abbeys are but two examples. Cistercians pioneered efficient farming, and as working communities survived by including within their number numerous lay brothers who helped run the monastery and the farms. It is not an exaggeration to say that the Benedictines (with the Cistercians) were perhaps more responsible

The ruins of Rievaulx Abbey

THE BISHOP'S CHURCH

Cathedrals within the Christian tradition represent a rather different strand. They take their name from the *cathedra* or bishop's throne, which stands at their heart. A cathedral is thus the church of the bishop, the focus of his teaching authority. Early on cathedrals would have been basilical in form, that is oblong with an apsidal (semi-circular) end. At the centre of this semi-circle sat the bishop flanked by his college of advisers, teaching his assembled flock. In Norwich, the eastern cathedra preserves this pattern, at the heart of a 'basilican' presbytery. Over the centuries the pattern of cathedral building evolved and many of them became cruciform (cross-shaped) in plan. Often this came about through association with a monastery. In England particularly, many of the cathedrals in the Middle Ages were administered by Benedictine monks. Worcester, Canterbury, Peterborough, Durham, Ely and Norwich are just some examples. In these cathedrals the prior ran the monastery and the bishop lived separately and was *de facto* the abbot. Other English cathedrals were secular from the beginning with a college of canons at their heart. Such was the case in York, Lincoln, Salisbury and at St Paul's Cathedral in London.

ARCHITECTURAL DEVELOPMENT

The style of architecture of English cathedrals and abbeys developed just as the communities who inhabited them did. The simplicity of Saxon architecture, often with fairly primitive round-headed arches and windows, gave way to the austere strength of the Romanesque style. Romanesque took its name from the solid round arcades and strong pillars which had developed from Roman architecture. In England this style is primarily associated with the Norman invaders and is often simply styled Norman. Durham Cathedral and Tewkesbury Abbey are two good examples from this period.

In the late-Romanesque period the arches began to become pointed and this style is often termed Transitional. In the late twelfth and early thirteenth centuries Romanesque gave way to the lighter touch of Early English, focused on the familiar three slender and parallel lancets seen at Rievaulx, at Whitby, or in the soaring elegance of Salisbury Cathedral. Early English marks the beginnings of mediaeval English Gothic which matured into the intricacy of the Decorated and Geometric tracery familiar in so many English parish churches. Among cathedrals York Minster is a splendid example, as is the nave of Beverley Minster. The apotheosis of English Gothic is reached in the Perpendicular period, during the fifteenth

The sumptuous fan-vaulting in St George's Chapel, Windsor

and sixteenth centuries, with its strong vertical lines and sumptuous fan-vaulting. St George's Chapel, Windsor and King's College Chapel in Cambridge are perfect examples. The nave of Canterbury Cathedral is another magnificent expression of the Perpendicular style.

The Renaissance led eventually to the rediscovery of the principles of Classical architecture, and the seventeenth and eighteenth centuries saw a flowering of the Classical style. The small city centre cathedrals in Derby and Birmingham are built elegantly in this manner and Wren's rebuilding of St Paul's in London is the most triumphant example of this style. In the nineteenth century mediaeval Gothic was revived; Truro Cathedral and the Anglican cathedral in Liverpool are both effectively born of this rediscovery of mediaevalism, albeit in a most creative manner. In some ways even Guildford and Coventry owe something of their origins to a modernised or transformed Gothic. Modernism has led to a far greater freedom of expression and different routes have been followed. The Roman Catholic cathedrals at Brentwood, at Clifton in Bristol, and at Liverpool testify to this variety, and it is to this myriad mixture of architectural styles and expression that this book seeks to introduce you.

Classical elegance in Derby Cathedral

Early English lancets in Salisbury Cathedral

THE NORTH

THE WISDOM of Aidan and the contemplative holiness of Cuthbert still linger in the atmosphere in the marches of the ancient kingdom of Northumbria. The Celtic mission is imprinted upon the landscape and although Lindisfarne, Whitby, Hexham and Ripon now boast buildings or ruins from a later age, the network of monasteries goes back to early times. The Normans took over many of the Celtic sites which had already found confluence with the Roman tradition through the Synod of Whitby.

At Mount Grace is the best preserved mediaeval Carthusian house. Rievaulx reminds us of Aelred and the Cistercian tradition, reflected also at Fountains Abbey and at Jervaulx Abbey, north of Richmond, and of the pioneering farming methods that were picked up throughout mediaeval England. Beverley, Selby and Carlisle offer a mixture of styles, and then in York Minster we see the apotheosis of English Gothic. It has the greatest wealth of mediaeval glass in England and the Five Sisters window with its grisaille colouring feels like one of the wonders of the world. All this is built upon the mixed Roman and Celtic traditions of Wilfrid and Paulinus. The Norman period which links this with the later Gothic is still visible in the minster's crypt, alongside the tomb of St William of York.

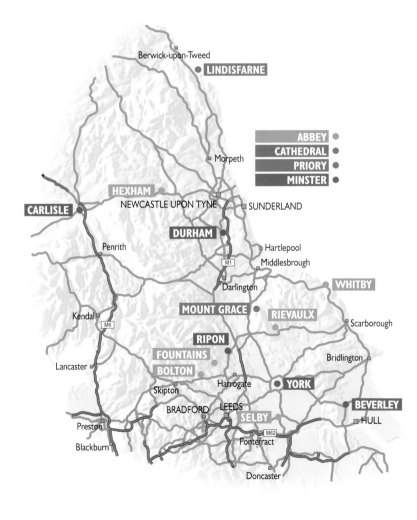

LINDISFARNE PRIORY

THE 'HOLY ISLAND' of Lindisfarne still retains that atmosphere bestowed upon it by the early Celtic saints who founded a monastery here. It was St Aidan who first came in 635, to found a church and a diocese close to the great royal fortress at Bamburgh. He travelled from Iona at the request of the Northumbrian king Oswald (who was also later canonised). Lindisfarne's aura of holiness increased with the reputation of St Cuthbert, the great Anglo-Saxon missionary bishop, who died and was buried here in 687. The Celtic monastery would have comprised simple wooden huts for the monks, grouped around the conventual church. In this early period Northumbria was one of the cradles of European Christianity, as the surviving evidence of the culture, notably

Lindisfarne, with the rainbow arch in the centre of the picture

St Cuthbert's Cross and the Lindisfarne Gospels, indicates.

Eighth-century Viking invasion destroyed the monastic church and the community fled. It was not until the twelfth century that the monastery was re-founded by the Benedictine community that kept Cuthbert's shrine in Durham; it is the remains of this church which can be seen today. Dominating the ruins is the splendid 'rainbow arch', one of the surviving ribs of the great stone vault over the crossing. Like Durham Cathedral, the church was vaulted in stone throughout and, also like Durham, the monks built the nave using alternate cylindrical and composite Romanesque columns. The church was begun around 1130 and the richly decorated western doorway and surviving south-western tower date from around 1150. The church was completed before the monastic buildings were begun (probably around 1200). The apsidal chancel was extended in the twelfth century to produce a square end; here would have been the high altar and possibly the shrine of St Cuthbert.

The building of the monastic complex began in the western range. The pattern of the monastery is still clearly discernible, grouped around the cloister garth. On the eastern side are the massive remains of the Prior's Lodging, fortified in the fourteenth century. The outer monastic court is still unusually well preserved. The site is stunning with the castle on an outcrop of the Great Whin Sill and the sands, covered at high tide, preserving the priory's island haven.

The great west window and remains of the monastic church at Lindisfarne

CARLISLE CATHEDRAL

Carlisle Cathedral: the tower with the north transept in the foreground

CARLISLE CATHEDRAL HAS seen perhaps greater ravages from a tempestuous past than most cathedrals; the truncated nave is the most obvious evidence of this. More cryptic evidence of its position on the frontier between England and Scotland is in the stones used originally either in Hadrian's Wall, or in the wall of the Roman city. All this adds to the cathedral's uniqueness, which is enhanced by it being the only mediaeval monastic cathedral to have been set within the context of an Augustinian rather than a Benedictine priory.

Viewing the cathedral before entering it, it is easy to appreciate something of its history. King Henry I founded the Augustinian priory and church of St Mary in 1122. In 1133 he carved a new diocese of Carlisle out of the See of Durham and so within ten years of its foundation the priory church became a cathedral. From the beginning it was cruciform in plan, and the remains of the nave are part of the earliest Romanesque building, constructed by Bishop Adelulf, the first bishop. The central tower was rebuilt by Bishop Strickland between 1400 and 1419.

The nave, converted into the Chapel of the Border

Detail from the great east window, Carlisle Cathedral

Regiment by Stephen Dykes Bower in 1949, still contains fine Romanesque arcading. The missing four-and-a-half bays were demolished during the Puritan Revolution between 1649 and 1652. The transepts are also Romanesque; the north transept forms St Wilfrid's Chapel and includes the Brougham triptych, carved in Antwerp around 1510.

Moving from the crossing into the choir, the architecture becomes Gothic. After a fire in 1292 destroyed much of the arcading, the remaining work was retained and supported by new piers. The splendid Decorated great east window parallels similar work at York Minster and Selby Abbey. The fifteenth-century stalls in the quire are very fine indeed; on the backs of the stalls in the south aisle, paintings tell the story of St Augustine, and in the north aisle that of St Antony and St Cuthbert.

Good evidence of the former monastery remains, in the Prior's Tower, Gatehouse, Tithe Barn and in the noble refectory (fratry) which became the chapter house in the seventeenth century. The modern treasury was completed and opened in 1990.

DURHAM CATHEDRAL

Durham Cathedral standing high on the bluff above the River Wear

THE VIEW OF Durham when approaching by train is unforgettable. A meander in the River Wear causes a stark outcrop of rock almost to form an island. This island is crowned both by the Norman castle and also by the magnificent strength and nobility of the cathedral. The origins of this great church (declared a World Heritage Site in 1987) lie further back still, in the gentleness of St Cuthbert's mission to the villages and farmsteads within the forests and wild moors of Northumbria. When Cuthbert died in 687 he was buried first on the 'Holy Island' of Lindisfarne. Three hundred years later, following waves of Danish invasions which necessitated the peripatetic movement of the saint's relics throughout Northumbria and the Scottish borders, Cuthbert's remains were reburied where Durham Cathedral now stands. Thus began the monastic life of Durham, which was later re-founded as a Benedictine community. Cuthbert's shrine remains the most sacred place in this stunning building.

Building began in 1093, when Durham was given palatine status by William the Conqueror, during the episcopate of William of St Calais. The cathedral – built for a prince-bishop who held temporal powers delegated by the monarch – contains undoubtedly the most consistent Romanesque architecture on this scale of any church in England. The main structure of the building took only 42 years to construct, though building continued throughout the twelfth century when the chapter house and Galilee Chapel were added. This western aisled chapel is the second most holy place in this remarkable building, for here is buried the Venerable Bede, who was the first to chronicle the history of the English people in his *Ecclesiastical History of the English Nation*. Bede drew together the complex threads which combined to form the story of the Roman and the Celtic missions to England; the cathedral's own history is rooted in this rich confluence of traditions.

The cathedral is approached from Palace Green, and entered through the north door with its splendid twelfth-century Sanctuary Knocker. The sheer strength and proportion of the building becomes immediately apparent when standing in the nave. The alternating composite and circular columns with their twisting 'barley sugar' decoration lead the eye up into the choir, and then beyond through the Neville Screen (1380) to the Shrine of St Cuthbert and eventually to the Chapel of the Nine Altars, which forms the easternmost part of the cathedral.

The nave, transepts and choir speak in essence of a consistent use of Romanesque architectural language. The forms used are sophisticated, with deeply recessed clerestory windows, bold decoration of the columns and the earliest rib vaulting in Europe. The four crossing arches each reach upward to 68 feet in height. The cloister and monastic buildings (including the vast Deanery) also owe their earliest form to the talent of Norman masons.

The story of the cathedral, however, does not end with the Norman builders. It was Bishop Richard le Poore who, in the period 1233–44, replaced a decaying Romanesque apse with a fine Gothic conclusion to the cathedral in the Chapel of the Nine Altars. Later on,

Alternate composite and 'barley sugar' columns in the nave of Durham Cathedral

The sixteenth-century clock in the south transept

Bishop Hatfield's tomb of 1333 would form the base of the loftiest episcopal throne in Christendom, later embellished with a seventeenth-century staircase and gallery. St Cuthbert's shrine is not the mediaeval original, which was lost at the Reformation; instead a stone slab is now crowned with a colourful tester by Sir Ninian Comper. The mediaeval screen between choir and nave was sadly removed in the mid-nineteenth century during a period of enthusiasm for openness. It was, however, replaced in 1876 by Sir George Gilbert Scott's marble screen, which remains there today and acts as a point of transition in one's journey towards the high altar and ultimately the shrine.

The outside of the cathedral is given strength and sense of proportion by both the massing of the Romanesque western towers which dominate the bluff overhanging the River Wear, and also by the stately and gently tapering nobility of Bishop Lawrence Booth's central tower; this was completed between 1465 and 1490. Within the building there are other unexpected features. The sixteenth-century clock in the south transept, remodelled in the seventeenth century, breathes a somewhat exotic presence in a building that elsewhere speaks of a refined austerity. Since the Reformation, the monastic buildings have been pressed into service in different ways. The monks' dormitory forms the museum, the monastic refectory has been converted into the library and, more recently, the undercroft has been made to house a restaurant and a permanent exhibition, 'The Treasures of St Cuthbert'.

HEXHAM ABBEY

THE ABBEY AT Hexham returns the pilgrim to the beginnings of English Christianity and to the origins of the Christian kingdom of Northumbria. King Oswald's victory at the Battle of Heavenfield, nearby, in 634 marked the start of a new era. About 674 Queen Etheldreda, the wife of King Egfrith of Northumbria, gave land to Wilfrid to build a monastery. Wilfrid, then Bishop of York, established a Benedictine foundation; the church later became the cathedral of the See of Hexham, lasting from 681 until 821. In 875 the monastery was pillaged by the Danes.

In 1113, Thomas, Archbishop of York, re-founded the abbey at Hexham as an establishment for Augustinian canons. The chancel and transepts are Early English in style and were constructed in the twelfth and thirteenth centuries. Of the Saxon building only the crypt now remains, and this can be compared with Wilfrid's crypt at Ripon Cathedral. There is also some evidence of the Roman occupation of Hexham in the stones of the

Hexham Abbey from the south

crypt and in the memorial at the foot of the night stair.

The abbey is entered through the slype – originally the passage between the cloister and the monastic cemetery. At Hexham, unusually, the slype is enclosed as the final bay of the south transept. Having entered the south transept and walked to the crossing, one can turn and view one of the wonders of Hexham in the stone night stair. This unique survival led the monks from their dormitory to the abbey church for the office of Nocturns, which was sung in the middle of the night. To the west is the nave rebuilt in Decorated style between 1905 and 1908 by the architect Temple Moore; at the centre of the nave is the entrance to the crypt.

The chancel dates from about 1180 and is entered through a unique closed wooden pulpitum with a loft built in the early sixteenth century by Prior Thomas Smithson. There are some fine misericords and two notable fifteenth-century chantry chapels. The Saxon frith stool, or Bishop's Throne, carved out of one piece of stone, is paralleled in England only by that in Beverley Minster.

WHITBY ABBEY

SET HIGH ON a cliff above the town, Whitby Abbey was known from early times as the 'beacon on the hill'. Its significance as a spiritual beacon can be traced to the year 657 when St Hilda, the first abbess, set up a double monastery for men and women. Hilda came from Anglo-Saxon stock and was taught by Paulinus, Bishop of York and missionary to Northumbria. Here, in 664, was the setting for the Synod of Whitby when Celtic and Roman traditions met and set a course for the future. Nothing is now visible of Hilda's monastery, which disappeared in Viking invasions in 867.

It was not until 1073–74, when Reinfrid, a monk from the abbey at Evesham, was sent north, that the abbey at Whitby was re-founded as a Benedictine monastery. In the years that followed a Benedictine church was constructed, following the traditional Romanesque pattern with an apsidal east end. The view which is most famous today is of the Early English east end which dates from the rebuilding that began in the 1220s. This aisled presbytery was built on a grand scale under the direction of Abbot Roger. The rebuilding included the choir with its splendid triforium resting upon Gothic arcades. The sheer

The noble Early English east end of Whitby Abbey

scale of the building drove the abbey into debt on more than one occasion. First of all, in the 1250s, the completion of the crossing and transepts crippled the monastery's finances. During the 1320s the abbey once again fell into debt as a result of the beginnings of a total reconstruction of the nave. The completion of this rebuilding had to wait until the fifteenth century with the construction of the great Perpendicular east window.

The remains of the monastery's domestic buildings are fairly sparse. The site of the cloister is clearly marked and there are some remnants of the outer parlour. The mediaeval prominence of the abbey is obvious in the scale of the ruined church. The cult of its many saints flourished during the Pre-Reformation period and it was this that enabled the community to rebuild the church on such a magnificent scale.

RIEVAULX ABBEY

IT WAS WALTER Espec, Lord of Helmsley, who brought a colony of Cistercian monks to establish their noble abbey in the narrow valley of the River Rye in 1132. Rievaulx was to become one of the most important Cistercian foundations in England and a great mission centre for the order. In 1147, the Northumbrian Aelred became abbot. Aelred was a theologian; he wrote about the monastic life and was an able administrator. Rievaulx's great church was

The great ruin of Rievaulx nestling in the Rye valley

built in two periods, during the 1150s and then during the 1220s. In Burgundian Romanesque style, the nave is of nine bays and originally was for the lay brothers, with the early-thirteenth-century presbytery of seven bays for the monks. The monastic ruins are very noble indeed, including a fine corner of the cloister arcade, and the foundations of the apsidal chapter house. Rievaulx's position is uniquely beautiful and the substantial ruins allow one to piece together the daily life of this the greatest English Cistercian centre of its day.

MOUNT GRACE PRIORY

TO VISIT MOUNT Grace is to encounter an expression of the religious life quite distinct from the community pattern seen in Benedictine and Cistercian monasteries. Here monks lived as hermits, but with some community worship. Mount Grace was founded in 1398 when the first aisleless church was constructed. In the 1420s the priory was expanded, the church was enlarged, a tower built, and the chapter house completed, along with the rebuilding of other monastic buildings.

Each monk lived in an individual dwelling. Happily one of these was reconstructed in 1901 when the manor house of 1654 (built by Thomas Lascelles) was rebuilt after the style of the 'Arts and Crafts Movement' by Sir Isaac Lowthian Bell. The dwellings were built on two floors, the living quarters on the ground floor and the workroom on the first floor. The dwellings were set around a great cloister, far larger than in other monasteries. The layout of these unusual communities is still clearly discernible from the ruins.

The later, ruined tower at Mount Grace

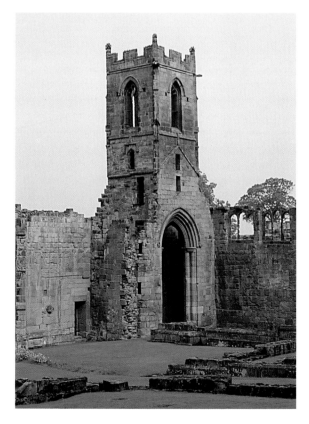

Ripon Cathedral

RIPON CATHEDRAL CAN rightfully claim to have the oldest fabric of any English cathedral, with the tiny crypt beneath the crossing dating back to 672, when it formed part of Wilfrid's church. Wilfrid, one of the most vigorous of the earlier missionaries to England, was a Northumbrian who embraced the Roman pattern of monastic life. Having travelled to Rome, he brought back to Ripon the ancient basilican pattern of church, with its semi-circular east end. Apart from the crypt, all of Wilfrid's church was destroyed in 950. The second minster, which replaced this, was also destroyed, this time by the Normans who, beginning in 1080, decided to build a more magnificent Romanesque building. The earlier foundation was Benedictine from Wilfrid's influence, but the later re-foundation was a college of secular canons.

Approaching the cathedral from the west, one first encounters the splendid Early English west front with its two rows of five lancets. This dates from 1220 as does the chapter house. The broad, aisled nave is Perpendicular in style; in 1450 the central tower collapsed causing significant damage to the minster – the present tower and nave date from around 1485, when the rebuilding began. However, King Edward VI dissolved the college of canons in 1547 before the rebuilding was finished; tell-tale signs of this are clear at the crossing where a Perpendicular pier links to an earlier Romanesque arch. The fine pulpitum screen also comes from this period of reconstruction, as do the earliest of the choir stalls and misericords, dating from 1494.

Ripon Cathedral from the east

The architecture from the crossing into the quire is in the Transitional style of the building commissioned by Archbishop Roger de Pont L'Evêque. This period of reconstruction effectively gave the minster its present plan. Further through the quire and to the south are the only remains of the Romanesque building of 1080, in the undercroft beneath the chapter house, now the Chapel of the Resurrection. There are some interesting furnishings in the cathedral, including a Tudor font, an art nouveau marble pulpit (1913) and a very fine eastern reredos of 1922, by Sir Ninian Comper, given as a memorial to the dead of the World War I.

FOUNTAINS ABBEY

IN THE QUIET valley of the Skell in 1132, Abbot Richard founded what was to become one of the greatest Cistercian abbeys in twelfth-century England. Even the ruinous buildings that remain capture the sheer scale of this vast monastery. The Cistercian life was reformed Benedictinism, pioneered in Burgundy in the early twelfth century under the leadership of St Stephen Harding at Citeaux and then by St Bernard at Clairvaux. It was a rule rooted in poverty, simplicity of life and isolation; the intention was to achieve self-sufficiency to avoid dependence on the worldliness of mediaeval society. Fountains Abbey, both in its location and its agricultural base, exemplified this well and it grew so rapidly that brothers were sent off to colonise eight new abbeys, five of which were in Yorkshire and nearby Lincolnshire.

To understand these ruins fully it is important to realise that the Cistercian life depended on vast numbers of lay brothers who helped run the farms. There were probably 600 lay brothers, and up to 120 monks. The great church had its origins in a smaller stone building completed between 1135–50; from 1150–1203 the abbey church was enlarged to accommodate the army of lay brothers. The style begins as Romanesque with a gradual transition towards the pointed arches of later Gothic. Despite the scale, the architecture still breathes Cistercian austerity with a restrained clerestory and no triforium. During the period 1203–47 the church was further enlarged and the eastern arm included a chapel of nine altars – a pattern copied a few years later in Durham Cathedral.

The monastic buildings reflect equally the size of the monastery and the Cistercian life that it sustained. The chapter house is one of the largest in England and the accommodation for the lay brothers is equally vast; within this complex is the fine vaulting of the cellar and lay brothers' refectory. Abbot Huby's majestic tower was built in the late fifteenth and early sixteenth centuries – such towers had been forbidden in the Cistercian orders in the early years of its foundation. These magnificent ruins bear testimony to the crucial influence of Cistercian life on mediaeval English society.

Fountains Abbey, with Abbot Huby's tower dominating the left of the picture

THE PRIORY CHURCH, BOLTON ABBEY

STANDING WITHIN A broad sweep of the River Wharfe, Bolton Abbey Priory has an incomparable setting. In 1155 Alicia de Romilly, of Skipton Castle, established an Augustinian Priory here, and in the ruins of the western part of the chancel of the old priory church, Romanesque blind arcading dating from around 1170, is still visible. Work ceased for fifty years and was resumed in the mid-thirteenth century with the construction of the nave in Early English style. The west front, which dates from this period, is highly ornate with a very fine west door. The most striking feature visible now is the incomplete western tower which was begun in 1520.

Bolton Priory ruins from the east

Work ceased at the Dissolution in 1539, and it was not until 1984 that it was roofed to form a western porch. The fine wooden roofing of the nave was begun by Prior Moone who was responsible for the western tower. The glass of six windows on the south is by Augustus W. N. Pugin and was inserted in 1853.

BEVERLEY MINSTER

BEDE'S *ECCLESIASTICAL HISTORY* refers to the monastery founded at Beverley by Bishop John of York. This monastery was re-founded as a collegiate church of secular canons in the tenth century and it gained greatly in significance with the canonisation of Bishop John as St John of Beverley in 1037. From the mid-eleventh century onwards the church was rebuilt in the Romanesque style.

Beverley Minster: the west front

Following a fire in 1188 and the collapse of the central tower in 1213, the church was again rebuilt starting around 1220. The new minster was conceived on cathedral scale, with double transepts like Lincoln. The rebuilding began at the east end with the fine Early English work in the retro-choir, choir and transepts. The nave was begun *c.*1311 in the Decorated style and completed in the 1390s; the Perpendicular western towers were added around 1400. Outstanding furnishings include the decorated tomb of Lady Eleanor Percy (*c.*1340), the choir stalls (*c.*1520) with 68 misericords, and the largest collection in England of carved figures playing mediaeval musical instruments. There is also a very fine Bishop's Throne.

Extensive restoration work was carried out on the interior of the minster during the eighteenth century and, again, the furnishings, including the font canopy and the carved panels on the inside of the west door, are superb.

YORK MINSTER

WHETHER ONE APPROACHES by rail or by road, the massive presence of the minster dominates the plain of York. The dominance of the city as a regional centre can be traced back as far as the third century when Constantine was proclaimed Emperor at York and there was a Christian community in the city. Paulinus' baptising of King Edwin, in 627, led to the building of this first church. Paulinus, the first bishop in York, was followed by Chad in 664 and Wilfrid in 669. York and its minster thus assumed great significance in England from the earliest Christian centuries onwards, contributing one man, Alcuin of York, to European history as organiser of education throughout Charlemagne's empire.

In 1075 Archbishop Thomas began to build a Romanesque church of sufficient size to fit the dignity of the city of York. Although it was called a minster (the Saxon word for monastery) it was always served by secular clergy and was never the home of a religious community. Under three later bishops – Thurstan, William Fitzherbert and Roger de Pont L'Evêque – the Romanesque building was completed. William Fitzherbert, bishop from 1145–47 and then 1153–54, was a Norman nobleman who found himself at the centre of controversy between church and king, which led to his ten year deposition. In 1227 he was canonised and became the centre of the modest cult of St William of York. Re-fashioned fragments of the Romanesque building are still visible in the crypt, near to his shrine.

The east end of York Minster from the city walls

Even this great Romanesque church was to prove inadequate to the dignity of York and it was in the time of Walter de Gray, the archbishop from 1215–56, and with his active support, that the building of the vast and noble Gothic church, that we see today, was begun. The north and south transepts were built first in the Early English style, including the incomparable Five Sisters window with its tall even lancets (the tallest in Christendom) and subtle grisaille stained glass. De Gray had set in motion a process of reconstruction which extended over a period of 250 years; his splendid tomb lies in the south transept.

The next stage of rebuilding was the construction of the chapter house from 1260–90 with its unique octa-pyramidal roof and flying buttresses – the architecture here is rather more delicate. From 1290–1360 the masons were set to work on the construction of the broad, majestic, aisled nave for which York is justly celebrated. The scale set by the nave and transepts would eventually transform York into the largest cathedral built in England during the mediaeval period. The treatment of the clerestory and triforium as part of one unfolding pattern is an innovative feature of the nave. The west front includes three large porticoes and the great west window, one of the chief glories of the minster. The presence of Parliament at York during the Scottish wars in the reigns of Edward I, II and III mean that both glass and statuary in the nave include the shields of the nobles of that time.

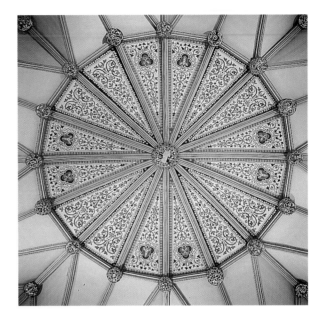

The chapter house ceiling

The great east window with its unusual double tracery

The rebuilding of the eastern arm of the minster was begun in the time of Archbishop Thoresby in 1361; this led to the final demise of the Romanesque building during the 1390s. This eastern work began with the Lady Chapel, built in sober Perpendicular with a magnificent great east window; the double tracery here covers an area the size of a tennis court and encloses the largest expanse of mediaeval painted glass anywhere in the world. Another triumphant feature of this part of the minster is the soaring eastern transept, with its windows running through to the full height of the choir roof. The central tower (which was intended to be completed with a further stage) was built between 1420 and 1430, and by 1465 the west front had been crowned with its two towers.

York Minster has not been without its dramas in modern times. In 1967 the entire structure was found to be in a precarious state of repair and a vast five-year conservation plan was initiated which included pouring quantities of concrete into the foundations; these concrete supports can still be seen under the central tower. The fire of 1984 destroyed the roof of the south transept; this has been meticulously and sensitively restored using traditional methods. Six of the roof bosses were designed by children in a competition organised by the BBC. Recently the great west window and the great west door have been totally recarved.

SELBY ABBEY

SELBY ABBEY IS built on slightly raised land in a low lying area prone to flooding; it thus stands out as a beacon from afar. The first abbey, begun by Abbot Benedict in 1070, was wooden; Benedict was later forced to resign and his successor Hugh began building the present stone church around 1100. Elements of this Romanesque building still remain. Hugh's vision took more than 130 years to complete and styles changed during the period of building. The abbey was established as a Benedictine foundation, but the monastic buildings disappeared at the Reformation.

Approaching from the west, the abbey is entered through the splendid Romanesque carving around the west door, and much of the lower west front dates from this period. On entering the nave the dominant style is again Romanesque with fine pillars decorated in the same fashion as those in Durham Cathedral. The earliest Romanesque work, and the oldest part of the abbey, is the west wall of the north transept – the north porch is also from the Norman period. By the beginning of the thirteenth century Early English patterns began to predominate and this is clear in the south nave triforium and in the upper levels of the west front. Much of the crossing has been renewed more than once due to two disasters. The tower collapsed in 1690, damaging the south transept and effectively destroying the adjoining chapter house. In 1906, following a fire, the choir roof collapsed and much of the crossing, transepts and nave had to be restored.

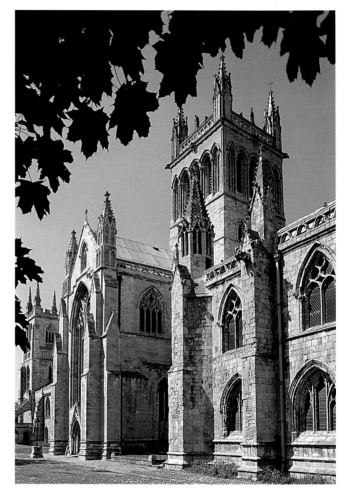

The Decorated choir dates from 1280, and this reconstruction concludes with the addition of the fine Jesse window of around 1330. In contrast with the flat wooden roof of the nave, the choir roof is a wooden vault with some fine gold bosses. The noble sedilia is thought to be by Henry Yevele, the king's mason, who built the nave of Canterbury Cathedral. The final stages of the western towers (probably intended by the Norman builders) were not completed until 1935, but they give an added dignity to the west front.

Selby Abbey from the south-east

Magnificent Romanesque carving around the west door

THE MIDLANDS

THE REGION described as the Midlands in this introduction to English abbeys and cathedrals, includes some places that might more popularly see themselves as 'northern' – Manchester and Liverpool are the obvious examples, but, even so, they are marked out from the far north and their expansion during the Industrial Revolution gives them a strong resonance with the area traditionally seen as midland England. The Christian church was established particularly early in Lichfield, and St Chad brought Celtic traditions with him. In the late eighth century, for a short period, Lichfield achieved metropolitan status, with an archbishop. The Norman hegemony in England can be traced in the splendid nave at Southwell Minster and also in the outstanding Romanesque frieze in the west front at Lincoln.

Otherwise Lincoln, one of the most magnificent ecclesiastical buildings of England, is a triumph of mediaeval Gothic, while outstanding contemporary architecture is displayed in the cathedrals in Liverpool and Coventry. The Anglican cathedral in Liverpool, monumental in scale, is the last Gothic cathedral to have been built and is triumphant. Its twin, standing on the same ridge above the city, is a complete contrast in its innovation and originality. Coventry Cathedral can boast works by a number of great artists of the twentieth century.

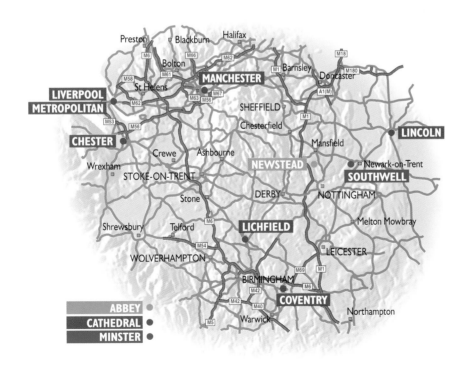

MANCHESTER CATHEDRAL

*Manchester Cathedral
from the south*

Set in the heart of a northern industrial city, it is easy to underestimate the historic roots of Manchester Cathedral. The attractive grouping of buildings comprising the cathedral and Chethams Hospital School are the direct descendants of the collegiate church established by King Henry V in 1421. The roots probably extend still further back, for, in 1871, when the greater part of the south porch was dismantled, an unusual carved stone was discovered, since known as 'The Angel Stone'. This probably came from the tympanum over the south door of the Saxon church of St Mary; the theme of the carving is the Annunciation.

The origins of the present church, however, are effectively from the early fifteenth century when it gained collegiate status. The quire and quire aisles date from this early period and were built by John Huntington, the first warden of the college and rector of the church. From

*The Fire Window in the
Regimental Chapel*

1465–81 the nave was rebuilt and Huntington's chapter house was completed around 1485. Within the nave the double aisles are an inheritance left by earlier chantry chapels, the screens of which were dismantled in the nineteenth century in order to open up the church to allow more seating. The church had become a cathedral with the establishment of Manchester Diocese in 1847. The quire chantries survived; these include the Jesus Chapel (1516) and the Regimental Chapel, founded as the Chantry of St John the Baptist in the early sixteenth century.

One of the most splendid features of the mediaeval fabric is the woodwork, with some excellent misericords, quire stall canopies and bench ends. The pulpitum screen is very fine as, indeed, is much of the work in the roofs of the quire and nave. Although the cathedral is substantially late mediaeval, there is some modern work. There were two significant restorations in the nineteenth century – the second helped redress some of the harm done in the earlier restoration and gave a new dignity to the building. The modern Lady Chapel replaces that destroyed by aerial bombing in 1940. There is a modern stone carving of the Christ Child by Eric Gill, five particularly fine stained glass windows by Anthony Hollaway, and the stunning Fire Window in the Regimental Chapel.

LIVERPOOL CATHEDRAL

Liverpool Cathedral, crowning St James' Mount, seen from the north-east

SIR GILES GILBERT Scott's Cathedral Church of Christ, in its magnificent position atop St James' Mount in Liverpool, is undoubtedly the triumph of twentieth-century Gothic.

The story of its construction over the period from 1904–78 mirrors the building of the great mediaeval cathedrals. Part of the achievement is the sheer nobility and scale of the building. Alongside this great sense of scale, however, Scott never lost sight of a concern for detail and decoration. The cathedral is dominated by the majestic Vestey tower, either side of which are the twin eastern and western transepts which enfold, on the north and south sides, the Welsford and Rankin porches.

To enter the cathedral from the west is to be almost overwhelmed with the impression of space, looking through the noble span of the nave bridge into the central space which allows enormous flexibility for worship. The arches enclosing it, which rise to 107 feet at their apexes, are the largest Gothic arches ever built. The space is beautifully enclosed by the transepts and porches. The transepts are variously conceived: one is the War Memorial Chapel, a second is now the visitor centre crowned by Keith Scott's sail-like aerial sculpture *The Spirit of Liverpool*, and a third contains the memorial to the earl of Derby whose support was so important in the early building of the cathedral. The fourth (the south-western) transept is the baptistry with its fine font of buff-coloured French marble surmounted by a soaring oak baldachino.

To the east is the high altar with its intricately gilded reredos including scenes of the Passion, Crucifixion and Last Supper. In the south choir aisle are the entrances to the Lady Chapel and its gallery. This was the first part of the cathedral to be completed (1910). Its more ornate style focuses the influence of G. F. Bodley who was appointed to work with the young Giles Gilbert Scott when construction began. A further glory of the building is the glass, crowned by Carl Edwards' splendid meditation on the Benedicite in the great west window.

Recent artistic commissions include paintings by Adrian Wizniewski and Christopher Le Brun, Elizabeth Frink's sculpture *Welcoming Christ* over the west door, and *Calvary 1998* by Craigie Aitchison.

Elizabeth Frink's Welcoming Christ *over the west door*

LIVERPOOL METROPOLITAN CATHEDRAL

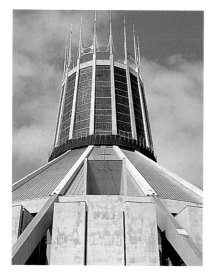

Liverpool Metropolitan Cathedral, showing Frederick Gibberd's revolutionary design

IN THE 1930s Sir Edwin Lutyens designed a monumental church to be built on a new site astride the same hill as Scott's Anglican cathedral. Only the crypt, however, with its notable six-ton circular 'rolling gate', was completed before the outbreak of war in 1939. Twenty years later Frederick Gibberd was appointed as architect for the cathedral and he used the crypt as a basic platform for his design. At the other end of Hope Street from Scott's great church, Liverpool Metropolitan Cathedral makes an eloquent ecumenical statement in this city of divided religious traditions. Crowning the city of Liverpool, it stands in complementary contrast to Scott's neo-Gothic building, and together they produce a dramatic skyline. Taking its cue from the liturgical movement, the cathedral's circular plan was revolutionary at the time. The lantern crowning the cathedral is a stunning sight both in daylight and at night, when it acts as a beacon on the city's skyline. The glass is by John Piper and Patrick Reyntiens, who had worked together earlier on the baptistry window in the cathedral at Coventry.

The interior of the great lantern by John Piper and Patrick Reyntiens

NEWSTEAD ABBEY

NEWSTEAD ABBEY WAS originally a priory for Augustinian canons, founded around 1163 by King Henry II. After the Reformation the buildings were acquired by Sir John Byron, ancestor of the poet, who converted them into a country house. However, elements of the priory survive, most notably in the cloister. There are also remnants of processional doorways, the lavatorium and the day stair.

The west front of Newstead Abbey house

The vaulted chapel to the great house was originally the chapter house in the priory. This dates from the mid- to late thirteenth century as does the west front of the priory church, the only part of the church still visible, and an example of a perfect Early English façade. A number of rooms in the house use the foundations of earlier monastic buildings and the present dining-room was originally the prior's parlour. In the salon, next to the fireplace, is a small section of painted wall decoration, the sole visible fragment of the monastic refectory dating from around 1200.

The western façade of the Priory Church

CHESTER CATHEDRAL

Chester Cathedral: the central tower

The Chapel of St Werburgh is in the north choir aisle, while her shrine still stands in the nearby Lady Chapel. The tower over the crossing is late mediaeval, but the corner turrets were added during the nineteenth century restoration by Sir George Gilbert Scott. The south transept, in contrast to its northern counterpart, is both larger and aisled and thus contains a series of chapels. There is a fine reredos in the Chapel of St Oswald by C. E. Kempe. Much of the monastic complex survives; the cloisters were largely rebuilt between 1525 and 1537. There is an unusual detached bell tower of 1975 by George Pace.

The fine choir stalls with their fourteenth-century misericords

THE ORIGINS OF Chester date back to around AD 79 when the Romans built a fortress on the River Dee. In the tenth century the remains of St Werburgh, a seventh-century Mercian saint, were brought to Chester to protect them from the Danes; Werburgh had been a nun and a great exemplar of the Christian life. Her relics were placed in a Saxon minster which was enlarged to house her shrine. After the Norman conquest the second earl of Chester re-founded the church as a Benedictine Abbey. St Anselm, Abbot of Bec in Normandy and later Archbishop of Canterbury, brought monks in 1092 to establish the abbey. After the Dissolution of the monasteries in 1541, King Henry VIII handed the monastery over to become the cathedral of the new diocese of Chester.

The Romanesque building took 150 years to build; only fragments of the Norman work survive, notably in the arches of the baptistry and in some of the arcading of the north transept. By the end of this period of rebuilding, styles of architecture had changed and transitional pointed arches began to emerge. This was clear in the monastic buildings around the cloister; the change of style prompted the second rebuilding of the abbey church itself in Gothic style. The beginnings of this can be seen in the Early English Lady Chapel of around 1275. The nave dates from the latter part of the fifteenth century. The choir is Early English of around 1200, though the splendid stalls with their misericords were probably carved in about 1380.

LINCOLN CATHEDRAL

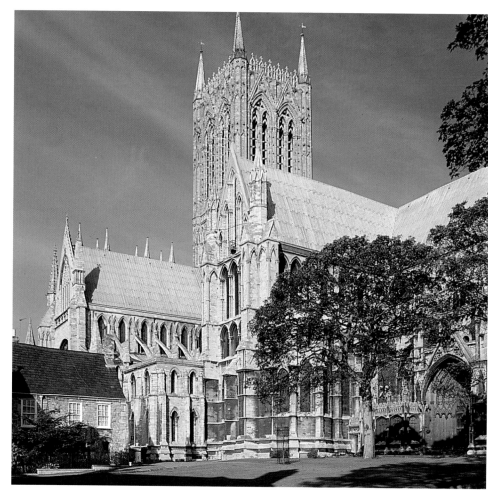

THERE IS PERHAPS no other cathedral in England in such a breathtaking position as Lincoln. Enthroned high on the limestone cliff that runs north to south through the county, it stands like a great ocean liner at anchor. Presumably it was constructed to dominate the vast diocese over which its bishop ruled. Like Norwich, Lincoln is an example of a cathedral being moved by the Norman conquerors to a strategically important centre. Bishop Remigius moved his see city here from Dorchester-on-Thames in 1072, only six years after the conquest. The west front of his cathedral has been preserved and, indeed, framed by the later Gothic work. Incomparable are the frieze panels of the flood and other biblical scenes; the whole frieze is being conserved and copies are being made to replace the most damaged original panels.

An earth tremor led to the demise of the Romanesque cathedral in 1185. It was St Hugh of Avalon, a Carthusian monk and a great mediaeval bishop, who rebuilt the cathedral, starting from the east. He kept the Norman towers and the great façade of Bishop Alexander as the sumptuous frame for the west door, to retain what John Ruskin described as one of the artistic wonders of Europe. Entering Lincoln through the great west door is in itself an enthralling experience. As the cavernous yet majestic interior opens up, the sheer scale on which the cathedral is built becomes apparent. The nave is not over-high, but it is both wide and long, with a mixture of limestone and Purbeck in its strong Gothic piers; the vaulting is plain but in scale with the rest of the nave which has relatively modest triforium and clerestory levels. The interior of the west front is distinguished by the lattice pattern in the stonework, said to be a trademark of one of the other great mediaeval builders of Lincoln, Bishop Robert Grosseteste.

The impressive size of the building can be appreciated from the crossing. The vaulting of the tower rises to 130 feet and the two transepts are themselves in proportion to the nave. At the end of the south transept is the Bishop's Eye, a fine circular window which looks out over the ruins of the mediaeval Bishop's Palace. Directly opposite, lighting the north transept is another circular window, the Dean's Eye, looking to the site of the earlier Deanery. Each transept has three chapels on its eastern side, and at the end of the south transept is a strong but sensitive sculpture of Edward King, the saintly and pastoral bishop of Lincoln during the latter part of the nineteenth and beginning of the twentieth century.

Beyond the elaborate fourteenth-century screen lies St Hugh's Choir, named in honour of its builder. The vaulting here is unusual with the asymmetry of the ribs. Some fine mediaeval ironwork opens out into the north-eastern and south-eastern

transepts. The north-eastern transept leads into the cloister. Here is a sure sign that Lincoln was not a monastic cathedral – monastic cloisters were built to the south to catch the sun. The northern walk of the cloister is enclosed by the noble and restrained library by Sir Christopher Wren. To the east stands the fine polygonal Gothic chapter house.

At the eastern end of the cathedral is the Angel Choir, the apotheosis of English Decorated Gothic, constructed as a means of housing the much visited shrine of St Hugh. In front of the shrine the paving is worn away through the constant kneeling of devout pilgrims. The Angel Choir is a daring conclusion to this majestic building with its trefoils, clustered pillars and angels reaching out from the higher levels. On the north side is the famous Lincoln imp, one of sixteen grotesques in the cathedral, which has become infamous through various attempts at popularism.

With its three vast towers, Lincoln dominates the city. The central tower, completed in the early fourteenth century, reaches a height of 251 feet. All three towers were surmounted by spires until the sixteenth century, with the central spire rising to a height of 524 feet. It was said to have been visible from East Anglia. The cathedral still crowns the county of Lincolnshire as a living and majestic piece of English Gothic.

St Hugh's Choir: the fourteenth-century woodwork

The rose window in the south transept, known as the Bishop's Eye

SOUTHWELL MINSTER

A VISIT TO Southwell Minster is an encounter with a number of unexpected delights. Set in the smallest 'cathedral town' in England, its two western spires are more reminiscent of Rheinland architecture. The historic roots of the minster can be traced to the establishment of a college of prebendaries in the mid-tenth century. The prebends' houses still remain, another unexpected gem within the tiny town. The collegiate status disappeared in 1841, but in 1884 the minster became the cathedral of the new diocese of Southwell. Remains of the palace of the archbishops of York can still be seen to the south of the cathedral.

Entering at the west end provides ample opportunity to admire the awesome strength of the nave, dominated by the drum-like pillars. Further down the nave are the noble Romanesque arches of the crossing, carved with rope mouldings. The two transepts are also Romanesque and provide further unexpected delights. In the north transept is an impressive eleventh-century tympanum which came from the earlier Saxon church. To the east of the north transept is the thirteenth-century Pilgrims' Chapel, refurbished in 1984 for the centenary of the diocese. From the crossing, the eye is drawn to the Perpendicular west window, the Angel Window, painted by Patrick Reyntiens, while Peter Eugene Ball's fine 1987 sculpture *Christus Rex* can be seen from anywhere in the nave. The splendid Decorated pulpitum of around 1340, with its vaulted vestibule and canopied stalls, leads into the choir which is built in a light Early English style. From the north choir aisle a passage leads to the magnificent late-thirteenth-century chapter house; built in the Decorated style and famous for its leaf carvings, it is the only octagonal chapter house in England with a stone vault unsupported by a central pillar.

The Airmens Chapel has a beautiful triptych of 1988 by Hamish Moyle, based on a poem by Edith Sitwell. A final delight can be found in the Vicars Court, at the east end, an elegant open quadrangle around which the Provost and canons now live.

The west front with its unusual double spires

LICHFIELD CATHEDRAL

THE ORIGINS OF Lichfield Cathedral lie in the building of a church in 700 as a shrine for St Chad. Chad, who was taught by St Aidan at Lindisfarne, was bishop from 668 to 672. In 1140 the Saxon church was replaced by Bishop Clinton's Romanesque building. This building had probably been started in 1085 and originally, in following the Norman pattern, it had an apsidal end to the choir. A larger church was begun in 1195, leading eventually to the completion of the present building in 1340. The choir, choir aisles, presbytery and central tower were completed in Norman Transitional and Early English style. The north and south transepts followed in 1220 and 1240 respectively; again the style is Early English and there is some elegant blind arcading. Unusually, the chapter house of 1249 is of two storeys, with the attractive central column

Lichfield Cathedral: the west front

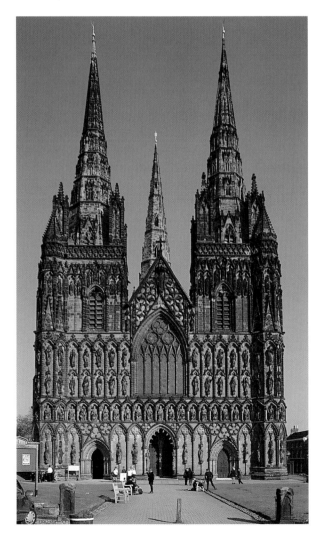

passing through both levels. The vestibule to the chapter house includes a fascinating feature, a place where on Maundy Thursday the foot-washing took place. There are thirteen seats where the poor whose feet were being washed would have sat. The greatest treasures of the library above the chapter house are the Lichfield gospels dating from around 735.

Lichfield Cathedral from the south-west, showing its distinctive three spires

In 1285 the present nave was completed in a Transitional style between Early English and Decorated. From the west end there is a splendid view of the entire length of the cathedral, since all the roof levels through to the Lady Chapel are at the same height. The west front with its twin spires was not finished until 1327. Finally, the Lady Chapel of 1330–40 was built in the Decorated style with its graceful lofty windows. St Chad's shrine was originally in this chapel, which meant, of course, that the Lady Chapel was the goal of mediaeval pilgrims. Originally the shrine would have been immediately behind the altar in the choir apse, but pressure created by the volume of pilgrims led to the extension of the cathedral giving a formal space (feretory) for the shrine. The shrine disappeared at the Reformation. In 1225 the Chapel of St Chad's Head was added on the south side. The skull of the saint was kept in a casket here.

COVENTRY CATHEDRAL

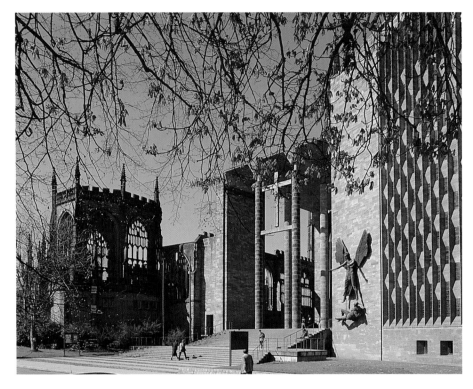

To visit COVENTRY Cathedral is to make a pilgrimage that is both unique and symbolic among all the cathedrals of England. It is profoundly moving to stand in the ruins of the old nave gazing upon the cross of charred timbers and the cross of nails with the two words, 'Father, Forgive'. The building of the cathedral caught the imagination of people throughout the world. It was seen as a phoenix rising from the ashes, offering itself to a continuing ministry of reconciliation.

The Christian roots of Coventry lie in the foundation of a nunnery by St Osburga. In 1043 Earl Leofric of Mercia and his countess, Lady Godiva, founded the Benedictine priory of St Mary which became the cathedral of the diocese of Coventry and Lichfield. With the establishment of the new diocese of Coventry, in 1918, the fourteenth-century Perpendicular parish church of St Michael became the second cathedral in Coventry's history. Following the destruction of much of the city through aerial bombardment in 1940, only ruins of this building remain.

Almost immediately after the blitz there emerged plans to rebuild, but it was not until 1956 that the foundation stone of Basil Spence's new cathedral was laid. Spence conceived his plan on the assumption that both the ruin and the new building formed a unity.

John Hutton's splendid western screen of engraved glass reinforces this feeling. The new building, of pink sandstone, is entered on the south side through a vast porch distinguished by the striking sculpture of St Michael and the Devil, by Sir Jacob Epstein. On entering the nave, the focus is Graham Sutherland's huge tapestry *Christ in Glory*, beneath which lies the Lady Chapel. On turning eastward the cleverly slanted nave windows, the work of Lawrence Lee, Keith New and Geoffrey Clarke, can be justly admired.

The baptistry window was designed by John Piper and made by Patrick Reyntiens; the Chapel of Christ in Gethsemane has a screen based on a crown of thorns, while the Chapel of Unity is a further symbol of reconciliation – this time between the different churches of the Christian tradition. In 1990 a statue, *Reconciliation* by Josefina de Vasconcellos, was placed in the ruins of the cathedral with an identical casting being placed in the Peace Memorial Park in Hiroshima.

Graham Sutherland's great tapestry of Christ in Glory

EAST ANGLIA

HISTORICALLY THE origins of the Christian Church in East Anglia are among the most fascinating in England. St Felix, a Burgundian, was sent by the Roman mission in Canterbury to found an East Anglian see. He did this in AD 633, probably at Felixstowe. Later the see moved to Dunwich, and then to North Elmham, Thetford, and finally in 1096 to Norwich. In the mid-seventh century, St Fursey brought a Celtic mission from the west coast of Ireland and set up a monastery within the walls of the abandoned Roman fortress at Burgh Castle, behind Great Yarmouth. Later in the seventh century St Cedd, a Northumbrian Celt, built a stone church – much of which remains – at Bradwell in Essex.

In later mediaeval times the Benedictine order left its marks. The largest church in East Anglia was the abbey church at Bury St Edmunds, the ruins of which lie near to the present cathedral; at Peterborough, Ely and Binham in north Norfolk, fine monasteries were built. Other orders left their mark – the ruined Cluniac priory at Castle Acre boasts one of the finest Norman façades in England. Generally, East Anglia is a very rich quarry for churches, abbeys and cathedrals – perhaps per square mile the richest in England.

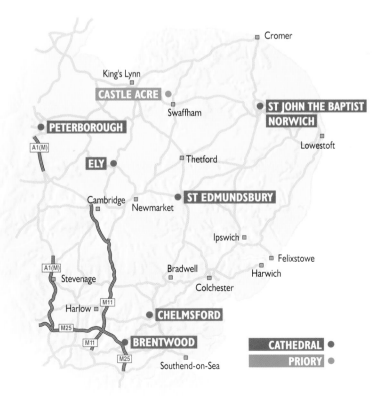

Norwich Cathedral

The view of Norwich Cathedral from above the River Wensum

AT 315 FEET Norwich's spire is the second highest in England, but it does not dominate the surrounding landscape after the manner of Salisbury. This is because Bishop Herbert de Losinga, on moving the see from Thetford to Norwich, chose to place the cathedral close to the heart of the existing town. This put the cathedral and priory on the edge of the marshy flood plain of the River Wensum. Remarkably, the 'footprint' of the monastic demesne established by Herbert in 1096 is almost exactly the same as that marking out the Close and cathedral precincts in the present day. It was in 1096 that construction began of the best preserved Romanesque cathedral in England. The floor plan still retains the apsidal east end, and in the nave the Norman architecture survives throughout the three levels from the floor, through the triforium to the clerestory.

There is much to be said for beginning a visit to the cathedral by walking up from Pull's Ferry, the watergate, to the Close. This Gothic arch on the riverbank betrays its original purpose as guarding the entrance to a canal which led up to the Lower Close. On this canal the Caen stone, ferried via Great Yarmouth and the River Yare, made its way to its final destination as the new cathedral took shape. On arriving at the Lower Close, to the right and bounding the eastern and northern sides of the green, it is still possible to see buildings set on the foundations of the old monastic bakery and brew-house and great granary. Next to the granary range stands the Prior's House, now the Deanery. This building retains some thirteenth-century work, including the Prior's Hall. Its south front, however, comprises a mixture of styles – Georgian, stepped Flemish gables, and also the mediaeval walls of the Prior's Hall. Until the nineteenth century there would have been buildings connecting the Deanery with the cloister and priory buildings. The cloister is entered from the north-east, through the old chapter house entrance. It is the largest monastic cloister in England and, following a fire in 1272, was rebuilt over a period of 150 years. The four walks offer one a graphic history of the development of English tracery.

The cathedral is entered by the monk's door, in the north-west corner of the cloister. The Romanesque nave, crowned by Bishop Lyhart's magnificent lierne vault, is an impressive sight as it stretches away in its record number of fourteen bays. Embellishing the nave vault are some of the cathedral's unique 1100 roof bosses. Starting from the crossing, these tell the Christian story of creation and redemption. The three easternmost bays of the nave form the choir, which is entered through Lyhart's pulpitum screen, surmounted by Stephen Dykes Bower's noble modern organ case. To the right, beneath the pulpitum, is the Chapel of the Holy Innocents, honouring all those, through the centuries, who have died innocently due to the cruelty of others.

The fifteenth-century misericords are very fine, and continue over the crossing. The strength of the Romanesque is nowhere more evident than in the shafts at the crossing, which bear the weight of the tower. Norwich was the tallest Norman cathedral tower and the unique patterning on the exterior probably dates back to the original masons and their work around 1100. The two transepts also contain

good Romanesque work at the higher levels, and particularly the north transept. The south transept was restored at floor level and on its southern façade by Anthony Salvin in the latter part of the nineteenth century.

The presbytery is an uncluttered Romanesque basilican space; the placing of the Bishop's Throne high up in the eastern apse is unique in northern Europe. The magnificent clerestory and vaulting is the joint work of two bishops – Bishop Percy in the fourteenth century and Bishop Goldwell in the fifteenth century. The delicacy of Bishop Percy's clerestory window tracery required Bishop Goldwell's masons to use flying buttresses to support the weight of the vaulting. The ambulatory, the almost circular St Luke's and Jesus Chapels, and the reliquary niche beneath the Bishop's Throne are again unique to Norwich. Now set in this niche is a modern icon of the Resurrection of Christ, a focus for prayer which reminds us of the holiness of this part of the cathedral.

The magnificent clerestory and vaulting is the joint work of two bishops in the fourteenth and fifteenth centuries

The nave and the interesting nineteenth-century west window

Outside the cathedral, to the east of the south door, is Life's Green where Edith Cavell, an honoured victim of World War I, is buried.

ROMAN CATHOLIC CATHEDRAL OF ST JOHN THE BAPTIST, NORWICH

THE ROMAN CATHOLIC Cathedral of St John the Baptist crowns one of the highest points in Norwich, and is a notable landmark within the city. It was built by the 15th duke of Norfolk who was also responsible for the fine Roman Catholic Cathedral in Arundel in Sussex.

Begun in 1882, the cathedral is the work of George Gilbert Scott and his brother John Odlrid Scott, and is in the Early English style. With its strong central tower it is conceived on a large scale with an aisled nave of ten bays and an aisled sanctuary. The north aisle of the sanctuary is a chapel dedicated to the Precious Blood, and the south aisle forms the Blessed Sacrament Chapel. The cathedral is cruciform and the triple lancet window in the north transept is said to have been designed by the duke of Norfolk himself. The first wife of the duke, in whose memory he gave the money for the cathedral, is remembered in the Chapel of St Joseph.

The Cathedral of St John the Baptist from the north-east

BRENTWOOD CATHEDRAL

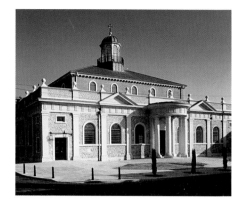

Brentwood Cathedral: the exterior

THE EARLIEST PART of the Roman Catholic Cathedral at Brentwood dates from 1861, when a parish church was built in neo-Gothic style. In 1989 work began on a building to adjoin the church and was completed two years later to a design by Quinlan Terry. The style is Classical, a mixture of early Italian Renaissance and Wren. The building is effectively a hall-like structure after the fashion of some of the City of London 'preaching boxes'. The Classical motif is carried through with great elegance and the retention of the Gothic Revival work adds to the interest.

Surmounting the Classical arcading are terracotta roundels. The climax of the building is a lantern, lit with round-headed clear-leaded lights; at the apex of the lantern is a dome and finally a cross. The bishop's chair and the ambo were both made in Pisa of Nabrassina stone. The cathedral is lit by brass Classical English chandeliers crowning the feeling of elegance and light. The Blessed Sacrament Chapel is part of the remaining 1861 Gothic Revival church.

The Classical interior with the Bishop's cathedra

CASTLE ACRE PRIORY

THE IMPRESSIVE RUINS at Castle Acre spring originally from the period of construction that followed the Norman Conquest and which included the building of Norwich Cathedral, Binham Priory and the priory in Thetford. William of Warenne, who is thought to have been the founder, arrived with William the Conqueror. He knew the great abbey at Cluny in Burgundy where the Cluniac Order began; the community followed the Benedictine rule but unusually came under the direct jurisdiction of the Pope. At its most prosperous the priory appears to have had more than thirty monks living within community. At Castle Acre the priory ruins include a fifteenth-century gatehouse, the twelfth-century west front, considerable evidence of the church and claustral buildings, and the modified remains of the Prior's Lodging.

The west front and Prior's Lodging, Castle Acre

The gatehouse is built of flint and brick and the Royal Arms, together with those of the Warenne and Fitzalan families (that of the duke of Norfolk), are all visible. The west front is magnificent; the main doorway is of four orders with elaborate mouldings and is set within the context of a triple series of blind arcades. The two examples of double arcading show a particular liveliness of feature and carving. Little is visible of the structure of the nave, except for the bay forming the south-west tower. Part of the sacristy survives with the remains of two Tudor fireplaces. The presbytery, originally apsidal, was later extended by three bays concluding with a square end.

Parts of the claustral buildings remain giving a fairly clear picture of the arrangements here. The monks dormitory and the reredorter (latrines), together with the refectory and infirmary, can all be identified. It is the modified remains of the western range which still dominate along with the west front. The Prior's Lodging, with its splendid oriel window, at one time took in the entire range and is still partially roofed. The porch has a pitched roof, added in the seventeenth century, when the building became a private residence after the monastery's dissolution at the Reformation; it is in an excellent state of preservation.

The great west door with its four orders of carving

PETERBOROUGH CATHEDRAL

The dramatic three portals of the west front and the later Perpendicular porch

THE WEST FRONT of Peterborough Cathedral with its vast Gothic triple portico is unique in Christendom. The roots of the cathedral lie in a monastery founded by Peada, the king of Mercia, in 655. This monastery, established by Northumbrian missionaries, would have followed the Celtic pattern; a survival from the Saxon period is the Hedda Stone in the apse, dating from around 780. In 870 the monastery was pillaged by the Danes, and the community came to an end. Later a new Benedictine community was established, and its abbey church was consecrated in 972, in the presence of King Edgar.

The present building was begun in 1118 following a fire two years earlier. By the year 1140, all of the Norman work east of the crossing was complete; the apse has survived along with arcading at all three levels. From 1133–78 work went ahead on the crossing, transepts and east end of the nave, all of which have retained their Romanesque purity apart from the insertion of Gothic arches on the E–W axis, when the Norman tower became unstable around 1335; the present tower is in the Decorated style. The west end of the nave is the work of Abbot Benedict,

and it is interesting that he continued the Romanesque design, even though by this time Canterbury, from where he came, was using French Gothic in its arcading. The splendid painted ceiling is unique in England and dates from about 1220. The western transepts, west front, and north-west tower were the last parts of the main cathedral structure to be completed around 1230.

The Perpendicular porch on the west front was built around 1380 to halt the forward leaning of the central arcade. The so-called 'new building', at the far east end of the cathedral, is of the richest Perpendicular construction and is by John Wastell, who was also responsible for the noble Bell Harry tower at Canterbury. Some of the monastic buildings survive, including the Almoners' and Infirmarers' Halls, the shell of the infirmary and hints of both the cloister and refectory. Among those who were buried in Peterborough Cathedral were Katharine of Aragon (1536) and Mary, Queen of Scots (1587), who was later reburied in Westminster Abbey.

ELY CATHEDRAL

The west front with the western tower and the south-west transept

THE 'SHIP OF the Fens' rising from the mist is an image often used to describe Ely's majestic cathedral. In earlier times it was not quite a ship, but certainly it crowned an island in the fens, an island famous for its trade in eels. To this island, in 673, came Etheldreda to set up her double monastery for men and women. Her shrine was at the centre of the earliest monastic church which was later destroyed by the Danes in 869. In 970 Benedictine monks re-established an abbey and in 1083, the octogenarian Abbot Simeon began building the Romanesque church.

Construction of the present church took more than 100 years to complete. The nave foundations were laid in the year 1100, and nine years later the abbey also became a cathedral. By the year 1106, the eastern end was complete and the north and south transepts followed. In the thirteenth century Bishop Northwold rebuilt the east end, adding six bays in the Early English style. The nave remains a good example of Romanesque work with a large triforium and rather simple clerestory. Two of the remarkable features of Ely Cathedral date from the fourteenth century. The splendid and spacious Lady Chapel was completed in the period from 1321–48 in Decorated style. It is the largest chapel of its kind attached to any British cathedral. In 1322 the central tower collapsed and the unique octagon was conceived by William Hurley, Edward III's master carpenter. The vast space crowned by the octagon was created by taking a bay from each of the four sides.

Sir George Gilbert Scott's board ceiling was built between 1855 and 1858. Few of the domestic

Ely Cathedral: the unique octagon

monastic buildings have survived – the chapter house and the cloister were destroyed at the time of the Dissolution, though, fortunately, the magnificent twelfth-century Prior's Door into the cloister has remained. Some of the monastic buildings, including the former infirmary, have been converted into domestic dwellings. The north-west transept, flanking the western tower, disappeared during the fifteenth century, but the western tower itself and the south-western transept remain as a noble west front welcoming the pilgrim and visitor.

ST EDMUNDSBURY CATHEDRAL

THE DEATH OF St Edmund, king of the East Angles, in the year 869 was clearly both a traumatic and formative event for this part of England. It is likely that he died close by to the present day town of Bury St Edmunds. In 1032 a round church was built as a shrine to house St Edmund's remains, which had been kept safely over nearly 200 years. The abbey was begun during the abbacy of Baldwin, 1065–97; he also built the nearby church of St Denis. Anselm, the abbot from 1121–48, continued the building, making the abbey church the greatest Benedictine foundation in East Anglia, larger even than the cathedral at Norwich. St Denis' Church was demolished to make space for the western transept of the new abbey church.

Anselm, however, also built a new church dedicated to St James, the nave of which was the antecedent of the nave of the present cathedral. In 1503 a new nave was built, the designer of which was the remarkable John Wastell who lived in Bury. Wastell was the builder of the Bell Harry tower at Canterbury, and the vaulting and ante-chapel of Kings College Chapel in Cambridge. His nave here at Bury has a similar sense of height and nobility. The present nave roof is by Sir George Gilbert Scott and the attractive colouring, designed by Stephen Dykes Bower, was added from 1948–82.

St Edmundsbury Cathedral from the south

It is to the genius of Stephen Dykes Bower that we owe the additions to St James' Church which were made necessary by its becoming a cathedral with the creation of the new diocese in 1914. His first new work was the north-west porch and the beginnings of the south walk of the cloister. In 1970 the crossing with its modest transepts and the fine aisled choir were begun. The style, which is twentieth-century Perpendicular, matches the nobility of Wastell's nave. Throughout, the ceilings are splendid in their colouring and there is a magnificent wrought iron screen at the entrance to the Lady Chapel. Plans are well advanced to complete the north transept and further cloisters according to Dykes Bower's plans, as well as a tower above the crossing designed by Hugh Mathew, his former partner.

The former abbey at Bury St Edmunds with one of the ruined crossing piers central to the picture

CHELMSFORD CATHEDRAL

Chelmsford Cathedral from the east

IN THE EAST of the diocese of Chelmsford, at Bradwell, stands the tiny church of St Peter. Built by St Cedd in the seventh century, it is the oldest stone church in England. This sets the context for the Cathedral Church of St Mary with St Peter and St Cedd in Chelmsford. Chelmsford gained its charter for a market in 1199, but the church of St Mary (as it was then known) came later; the first named incumbent is Richard de Gorges, who was presented to the living in 1242. No fabric from this early period is visible since the church was rebuilt in the fifteenth century as the significance and dignity of the town had increased. The western tower is fifteenth century, the lantern and needle spire being added in 1749. The two-storeyed south porch is also fifteenth century, but the mediaeval nave collapsed in 1800 when it was rebuilt, still in Gothic style and with galleries that were later removed.

The whole cathedral was extensively reordered and refurbished in 1983 when it gained its present feel of grace and space. A new limestone floor was laid and a Westmoreland slate altar (by Robert Potter) and bishop's chair (by John Skelton) were placed in the graceful fifteenth century chancel with its slender arches looking north and south into the aisles. The church became a cathedral in 1914 with the creation of the new diocese of Chelmsford, and a modest extension was added to the chancel in the 1920s. There is more modern work at the west end in the chapels of St Peter and St Cedd. St Cedd's Chapel is set aside for private prayer; outside the screen on the north wall is a relief, *Christ the Healer*, by Georg Ehrlich. Another Ehrlich relief, *The Bombed Child*, can be seen in the Chapel of St Peter. It reflects the dedication of the chapel to those who suffer 'in this world'. The chapter house was built in 1990. Two fine organs, built by N. P. Mander in 1994 and 1995, are the most recent additions to this modest but most elegant of cathedrals.

HEART OF ENGLAND

For many, the western counties that border the Welsh Marches represent the quintessence of English countryside and architecture. Reaching down into Gloucestershire and Oxfordshire, the honey-coloured Cotswold stone sets the scene. On any reckoning, Gloucester would find its place among the 'top ten' English cathedrals. Its Romanesque work is matched by the strength and nobility of the great abbey at Tewkesbury, just a few miles to the north. In some ways, in the Middle Ages this was the very heart of England, for Hailes Abbey with its celebrated relic of the 'holy blood' was a centre of pilgrimage which vied with Canterbury and Walsingham for popularity.

The winding course of the great River Severn, passing by Gloucester, takes us on to the cathedral at Worcester, which owes much to the saintly Bishop Wulfstan and was originally a Benedictine foundation. Hereford had no monastic origins, but became a centre of pilgrimage with the shrine of St Thomas Cantilupe as the focus of devotion. Christ Church, Oxford, was monastic in its foundation and then later also became the chapel of the magnificent college re-founded by Cardinal Wolsey in the sixteenth century. The abbey church at Dorchester-on-Thames was the original centre of the largest diocese in England, whose centre later moved to Lincoln.

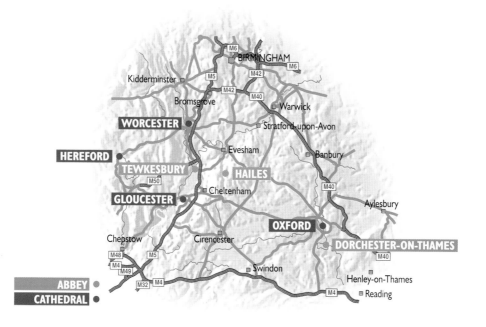

WORCESTER CATHEDRAL

WORCESTER CATHEDRAL, STANDING proudly above the River Severn, is a symbol of this part of England. The diocese has a long history; the first bishop was Bosel, in 680. By the year 983, the cathedral had been established by Bishop Oswald. In 1041 the cathedral was seriously damaged in a Danish raid, but it was not until 1084 with the general initiative of William the Conqueror that Bishop Wulfstan began the rebuilding. This was started from the east end, and by 1089 the crypt and the area above it was complete, this crypt has survived and it remains the largest Norman crypt in England. Building continued until the Romanesque cathedral was complete. The two western bays, finished around 1170, are late enough to be in the Transitional style.

Wulfstan's achievement was considerable and he was canonised in 1203. During the thirteenth century, King John was buried in the cathedral (1216) and his noble tomb remains at the centre of the quire. In 1224, Bishop William de Blois, began rebuilding in Early English style, beginning with the new Lady Chapel at the east end, in Early English style. He continued to rebuild, moving west through the quire and demolishing Wulfstan's Romanesque cathedral. This work continued throughout the fourteenth century, with a break

almost certainly caused by the Black Death. This break is detectable since the earlier work is Decorated, while the later southern arcades of the nave are Perpendicular in style. The tower and great transept were completed, also in the Perpendicular style, by 1374.

Worcester Cathedral: the tower and west end

The north porch was completed in 1386 and the remarkable and elaborate chantry to Prince Arthur, the older brother of King Henry VIII, was completed in the period after his death in 1502. Amongst the monastic buildings to survive is the chapter house with its banded green and white stone and one central supporting column, and also a fine cloister rebuilt at the end of the fourteenth and the beginning of the fifteenth century. Recent excavation has revealed a substantial wall concentric with and encircling the chapter house, either contemporary with it or perhaps from an earlier period. At the Reformation the monk's refectory survived and became College Hall which is now used by the King's School.

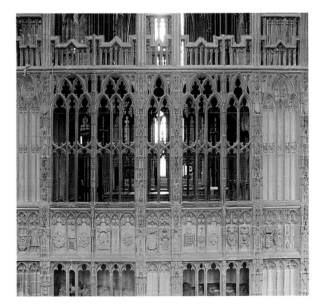

The south elevation of Prince Arthur's chantry chapel

HEREFORD CATHEDRAL

The cathedral seen from across the River Wye

The splendid dignity of the central tower owes its origins to the fourteenth century and notably to the gifts received from pilgrims, following the canonisation of St Thomas Cantilupe in 1320. Cantilupe was a pious, learned and courageous bishop. He defended his own diocesan jurisdiction in the face of John Peckham, Archbishop of Canterbury, and indeed died while still excommunicated by the Primate.

The fifteenth century saw the construction of the delightful college of the Vicars' Choral in 1475. The only surviving parallels to this beautiful collection of buildings overlooking the River Wye are at St George's Chapel, Windsor, and Wells Cathedral. In 1480, the splendid fan-vaulted Stanbury Chantry was completed. The eighteenth and nineteenth centuries saw substantial restorations. James Wyatt rebuilt the west end of the nave following a collapse in 1786, and the Victorian restoration dates from 1830–70. Hereford has some remarkable treasures including the Mappa Mundi (*c.*1290), the Limoge reliquary, the Anglo-Saxon Hereford Gospels and the Chained Library, the furnishing of which dates from 1611. These treasures are now housed in the refurbished cloister and in a fine new library building designed by Sir William Whitfield and completed in 1996.

THE BEGINNINGS OF the diocese and cathedral at Hereford take us back to the year 676 when a stone Saxon church replaced the old wooden structure dedicated to St Mary the Virgin. In the next century both a library and school were probably established together; King Offa of Mercia was a patron of Hereford at this time. The Normans rebuilt the cathedral and substantial elements of this Romanesque building have survived including the south transept, much of the crossing and choir, and the main aisle of the nave.

In the thirteenth century the next significant developments came when the cathedral was transformed with the introduction of Early English work. An ambulatory was built at the eastern end, together with a Lady Chapel constructed over a crypt, unique at this time in England. The north transept was built around 1250, using Purbeck marble and acute Gothic arches mirroring those in Westminster Abbey, which date from the same period. A ten-sided chapter house was also built at this time, the ruins of which can still be seen.

The cathedral nave looking westwards from the choir

TEWKESBURY ABBEY

TRADITION SUGGESTS THAT a Saxon Benedictine monastery was founded at Tewkesbury in the early part of the eighth century. The present building traces its origins to the Norman re-foundation by Robert Fitzhamon in 1087. Tewkesbury is undeniably one of the great Romanesque buildings of England. Outside there is much to admire, including the noble recessed Norman arch in the west front, and the massing of the central tower, the largest Romanesque tower in England. Inside the building, the nave echoes the Norman origins of the church, consecrated in 1121, with its dominating circular columns. The choir and transepts (from this period) were almost certainly the earliest four-storey buildings in Europe. Two-thirds of the way along the nave is a shallow step crossing the entire width of the church. This is the only evidence of the screen that would have divided the nave from the monastic choir. The Lady Chapel is a perfect example of a Romanesque apsidal chapel, and there would have been a similar chapel originally in the north transept.

In the thirteenth and fourteenth centuries, the De Clare family left a clear and unforgettable mark upon this splendid building: The choir and presbytery were rebuilt in the Decorated style and fine lierne vaults were added (1310–40) to both nave and chancel. The Romanesque pillars were reduced to half their original height and used as the basis of this new work. Some of the early abbots are buried in the south ambulatory, including Abbot Alan from whom we learn most of our first-hand knowledge of the martyrdom of St Thomas Becket. In this same period the chevet of chapels at the east end were added. The fine chantry chapels for the Despenser, Fitzhamon and Beauchamp families date from 1390 and 1425. The Despenser Chapel is an early example of fan-vaulting and it includes some fragmentary gold-leaf painting on the east wall. The Beauchamp Chapel is the latest and most magnificent of the Tewkesbury chantries, again displaying some sumptuous vaulting. The monastic buildings were largely to the south of the present church but these disappeared with the advent of the Reformation, and now only the Abbot's gateway remains.

Tewkesbury Abbey from the north-west

GLOUCESTER CATHEDRAL

Gloucester Cathedral from the south-east

GLOUCESTER CATHEDRAL IS a building of dramatic contrasts and dazzling beauty. The contrast between the clear robust splendour of the Romanesque nave and the intricacy of the Perpendicular choir, presbytery, tower and Lady Chapel is unforgettable. The origins of the cathedral reach back into the seventh century when King Osric of Mercia established a monastery here in 679. During the reign of Cnut, the monastery was taken from the secular priests and handed over to Benedictine monks. It was the arrival of the Normans, however, that presaged the building of the earliest parts of the cathedral which are still visible today. The foundation stone of the new abbey church was laid in 1089. In 1541 King Henry VIII founded a new diocese and the abbey became a cathedral.

The fine Romanesque nave was not completed until around 1126. The architecture is simple without being severe, robust and yet still graceful. The strong and plain circular columns reflect a pattern resonant with other churches in the Severn valley. The decoration of the arches is in the restrained dog-toothing patterns characteristic of Norman work; the triforium above is low, owing to the scale of the main arcades. During this period there was internecine strife between the sons of William the Conqueror. Robert Curthose, the eldest son, who had hoped to succeed to the throne, was held captive in Cardiff Castle for many years and eventually buried here in the chapter house of the Abbey of St Peter, Gloucester. His wooden effigy is now in the south ambulatory of the choir. The

Romanesque nave is crowned with a beautiful plain Early English vault of 1242.

Gloucester preserves the clear patterns of the former Benedictine monastery perhaps better than any other English cathedral, since many of the pre-Reformation monastic buildings survive. This is true too of the church itself. The clear division between the nave, or people's church, and the choir, or monks' church, is still there in the early-nineteenth-century choir screen. To move into the choir and presbytery is to move into a different world, not only in terms of monastic origins but with regard to the architecture, for the choir, transepts and presbytery are examples of the earliest and most beautiful Perpendicular work in England.

The Norman east end would have been fairly dark, and the vaulting, windows and tracery, built after the murder of Edward II, whose majestic tomb is in the north ambulatory, give a feeling of light, space and height. The great east window is one of the wonders of Gloucester. It is effectively a great glass reredos depicting the mediaeval hierarchy with angels in the top panels, Christ, Mary and the saints in the upper ones, and knights and bishops at the bottom. Many of the knights commemorated fought at the Battle of Crécy of 1346. In contrast to this mediaeval glass, nearby in the south ambulatory is the fine Thomas Denny window of 1993, picturing the Risen Christ. There is also some good nineteenth-century glass by C. E. Kempe on the north and south sides of the ambulatory. The lierne vaulting of the presbytery is covered with bosses and this part of the cathedral reaches remarkable conclusions in both the east and

Part of the great east Crécy window

the west. In the west, flying spans carry the springing for the last bay of the vault. In the east there is a passage linking both the north and south sides, known as the Whispering Gallery. This also acts as an extraordinary bridge to the Lady Chapel.

The Lady Chapel, begun in 1470, is a stunning conclusion to the building. It is unusual in having chantry chapels to both south and north with singing galleries above them. The chantries have fan-vaulting but the Lady Chapel itself has a lierne vault similar to that in the choir, with parallel ridge-ribs. The chapel, which was badly damaged after the Reformation, contains magnificent glass by the 'Arts and Crafts' artist Christopher Whall, completed in 1905. His daughter made the St Christopher window on the south side above the singing gallery, in memory of him in 1926.

The magnificent Perpendicular great cloister is considered by many to be the most beautiful in England

The great cloister is arguably the most beautiful cloister in England. It was begun in the 1360s and completed very early in the fifteenth century and the fan-vaulting is one of the glories of this period. The tower, also Perpendicular, is from the mid-fifteenth century.

HAILES ABBEY

WHEN IN 1270 Edmund, son of Richard, Earl of Cornwall, presented a phial of the Holy Blood to Hailes Abbey, he transformed the monastery into one of the most celebrated pilgrimage centres of mediaeval England. Hailes had been founded twenty-five years earlier as one of the last Cistercian houses in England, through the gift of the manor of Hailes by King Henry III to his brother, the earl of Cornwall. The monastery was completed in Cistercian style around 1255, with a four bay presbytery and an eight bay nave, the last five bays of which were for the lay brothers.

The arrival of the holy blood led to the rebuilding of the east end of the presbytery with a corona of chapels, a 'chevet' to house the shrine. Of the monastery, only fragments of the ten-bay cloister remain; otherwise little of the abbey survives above ground. The cloister ruins include some fifteenth-century rebuilding, with just some small evidence of the window tracery.

Hailes Abbey: looking through the ruined cloister arcade

DORCHESTER ABBEY

DORCHESTER ABBEY'S ORIGINS lie with the baptism of the pagan king Cynegil by St Birinus in AD 635. The see later moved to Winchester, but in 869 Dorchester became the cathedral of the largest diocese in England, stretching from the Thames to the Humber; in the 1070s the Normans moved the bishop's seat to Lincoln. The abbey was re-founded as Augustinian in 1140, with a fine cruciform church at its heart. The monastic buildings have disappeared, except for the abbey guest house, but the superb church remains.

Dorchester Abbey from the south-west

The east end of the church was re-modelled in the Decorated period with fine tracery in the great east window. The sedilia in the sanctuary anticipates the Perpendicular style with its pinnacled canopies. The Tree of Jesse window in the north is unique and overlooks the Chapel of St Birinus. which was built around 1320 to house the shrine. The chapel contains a beautiful roundel depicting the blessing of St Birinus by the archbishop. On the south side, the People's Chapel, built as a parish church around 1340, was originally divided from the monastic church by a screen along the arcade.

The roundel in the Chapel of St Birinus is the earliest glass in the abbey, dating from 1225–50

CHRIST CHURCH CATHEDRAL, OXFORD

CHRIST CHURCH, OXFORD, is unique among English cathedrals inasmuch as it serves both as a cathedral and as a college chapel. The cathedral is approached from St Aldate's through the magnificent Tom Quad started by Cardinal Wolsey, and with the noble Tom Tower added by Sir Christopher Wren in 1682; to make way for this the priory church (now the cathedral) was substantially foreshortened. Although the building is comparatively small it is nevertheless a treasure-house both historically and architecturally. In the early history of the cathedral the legend of St Frideswide dominates. It is not known for certain whether she founded the monastery that preceded the later Augustinian foundation; her death in October 727, however, is attested from the twelfth century, and her burial place was probably in or near the north-eastern side of the present cathedral, to the north of the present grave slab. The origins of Oxford can probably be traced to this early Saxon nunnery, which was eventually burned to the ground in 1002 by the Danes. The church was rebuilt in the year 1004 by King Aethelred, who had a manor in Headington to the east of Oxford.

The cathedral from Christ Church Meadow

At the beginning of the twelfth century the monastery was re-founded as a priory for Augustinian canons. In the third quarter of that century, the then prior, Robert of Cricklade, established the plan of the present church, chapter house and cloister. His chancel was finished in 1170 and the tower at the crossing, with its aisled transepts, was finally completed about fifteen years later. The cathedral spire (one of the earliest in England) dates from around 1230, as does the Lady Chapel. The Latin Chapel dates, in its completed form, from 1338.

One of the glories of the cathedral is William Orchard's superb lierne quire vaulting with its elegant pendants (*c.*1500). The only other monastic buildings to have survived are the Prior's Lodging and parts of the old dormitory and refectory (now Priory House). The fine Early English chapter house dates from 1220–40 and has some splendid interior carving. The stained glass is of great variety, much of it dating from the fourteenth to seventeenth centuries; in the Latin Chapel there is some glass by Sir Edward Burne-Jones.

LONDON AND THE SOUTH EAST

AUGUSTINE'S ARRIVAL in Kent in AD 597 marked the beginnings of the English Church as it exists today. Not only did Augustine build a cathedral, he also established the abbey nearby, which bears his name. The advance of his mission to Rochester and then to London led to the beginnings of Rochester Cathedral and St Paul's Cathedral in London around 604. This part of England, however, bears the marks of an even earlier Christian mission with the martyrdom of St Alban early in the third century.

Battle Abbey in Sussex reminds us of the Norman invasion of Britain which left its mark upon a number of English cathedrals and abbeys, not least in the South East. The transepts in Winchester, the east end of Canterbury and parts of St Albans and Rochester are obvious examples. The royal Benedictine foundation of Westminster Abbey predates the Norman conquest in its origins; it survived the Reformation with a number of the monastic buildings intact. There is also some interesting architecture from more recent times, notably in the splendid neo-Byzantine Westminster Cathedral and in the modernised Gothic of Guildford Cathedral. London's focal position makes it an ideal centre for exploring something of the spiritual, architectural and cultural history of South East England.

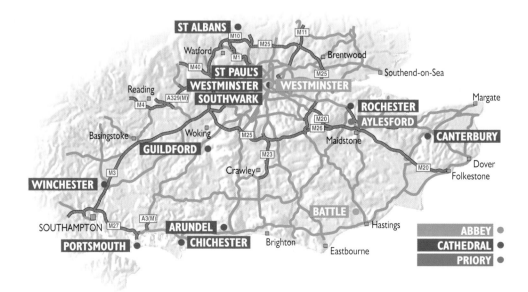

ST ALBANS CATHEDRAL

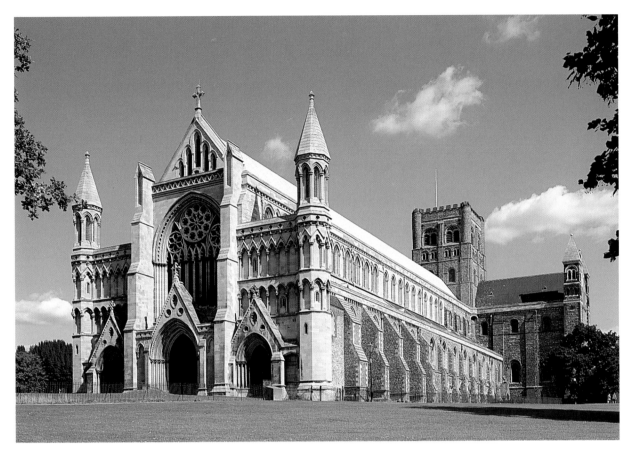

THE STRONG AND austere tower of the Cathedral and Abbey Church of St Alban, boasting Roman brick in its construction, focuses the unique interest of this historic place. Here, outside the ancient Roman city of Verulamium, in the mid-third century, Alban became the first Christian martyr of this land. There was a shrine here as early as 429, and in the eighth century Bede wrote that here 'a beautiful church worthy of (Alban's) martyrdom was built.' In 793 King Offa of Mercia established a Benedictine double monastery and in 960 it was re-founded with a stricter Benedictine discipline.

The present church was begun in 1077 and from the beginning the monastery was conceived on a grand scale. All that now remains following the dissolution is the gatehouse and the abbey church. Approaching from the gatehouse it is easy to appreciate both the scale, and significance of Lord Grimthorpe's nineteenth-century restoration, when the west front was completely rebuilt. The nave at 275 feet long is the longest in England. Inside the four western bays were extended in 1190 in Early English style, while the easternmost arcades are Romanesque with plaster covering Roman

brick. After their collapse in 1323, the four bays of the south nave were reconstructed in the Decorated style.

The long nave of St Albans Cathedral seen from the south-west

The nave is separated from the choir and presbytery by a stone screen, beyond which is the monk's church. The choir and transepts include much Romanesque work, but the end wall of the south transept was rebuilt in the 1880s. Beyond the fine high altar screen of 1484, restored by Lord Aldenham in the 1890s, is the shrine of St Alban. The pedestal of the shrine, dated 1308, was magnificently restored in 1991. Still further east is the Lady Chapel, built during the period 1257–1320. For 300 years it was walled off from the rest of the cathedral and used by St Albans School.

The glory of the twentieth-century additions to the cathedral is the chapter house, designed by Sir William Whitfield using modernised Romanesque forms and opened in 1982. It includes a library, song school and refectory, and the choir now progress into the cathedral from the chapter house using the Michael Stair, a dramatic gallery and staircase modelled on a mediaeval 'night stair'.

St Paul's Cathedral

The west front of St Paul's Cathedral

Augustine's mission to Kent in 597 meant that in England, following the Roman pattern, dioceses began to be set up based in established cities, with Celtic cathedrals often in wilder countryside. So, only seven years after Augustine's arrival, Mellitus adopted this pattern and established the first church of St Paul in London in 604. It was a wooden building which was destroyed and rebuilt several times before a Norman church was constructed on the same site nearly 500 years later, in 1087. This church eventually evolved into the great gothic building that preceded Wren's

masterpiece. Old St Paul's was the largest church in the British Isles and the third largest in mediaeval Europe, with the tallest spire ever built in England; even the tower pillars, which Wren had to demolish, were more than 200 feet high. The Great Fire of London in 1666 finally put paid to the decaying building.

The design of Christopher Wren's new cathedral reflected the contemporary interest in Classical architecture and was built in English Baroque. It was constructed between 1675 and 1710 and is dominated by the magnificent dome, which is 365 feet high to the top of the cross which surmounts it. The dome itself has become a symbol of the city of London. The cathedral was built using stone from the royal quarries at Portland in Dorset. The west front has a pediment which includes a bas-relief of the conversion of St Paul, and this pediment is crowned with a statue of the saint flanked by figures of St Peter and St James. The twin towers of the west front house the bells and the clock, including the largest bell, Great Paul, which weighs 17 tons.

The cathedral is entered through the west front, having passed, at the bottom of the steps, the statue of Queen Anne (the reigning monarch when the cathedral was completed). The building is broad and cruciform in plan. The view down the wide nave and beyond the crossing is rich and splendid, with the fine mosaics on the ceiling of the quire, and the great baldachino fixing one's gaze on the far distance. The broad Classical arcading of the nave breathes an atmosphere of splendour and strength. The nave is flanked by north and south aisles. In the north aisle is Alfred Stevens' towering monument to the Duke of Wellington; at the far west end is the Chapel of St Dunstan decorated after the manner of Raphael. The south aisle has as its western-most chapel that of the Order of St Michael and St George, an order with strong links with the diplomatic service.

Moving further east, the transepts are again broad. In the north transept is the Italian marble font which dates from 1727. Also here is one of the three versions of William Holman-Hunt's famous painting *The Light of the World*. In the south transept is John Flaxman's monument to Admiral Horatio Nelson, whose tomb is in the

The magnificent nave looking to the crossing and choir

A view of the dome from the interior

centre of the crypt. The dome encloses a vast space at the crossing, which is paved in black and white marble and at the centre is the Latin epitaph to Wren which includes the famous phrase: '..... if you seek his monument, look around you.' The dome is among the largest in the world and, high up but still below the windows, is the famous 'Whispering Gallery'. The frescoes inside the dome, depicting the life of St Paul, were painted by Sir James Thornhill between 1716 and 1719.

The magnificent baldachino in the choir is modern (1958) and surmounts an altar of Italian marble; this replaces earlier work lost through bomb damage. The very fine choir stalls are, like much of the other carving, the work of the seventeenth-century Dutch master, Grinling Gibbons. In the ambulatory is Henry Moore's fine modern sculpture *Mother and Child*. Finally, descending to the crypt, we enter another remarkable world. It is the largest crypt in Europe and, despite its size, it is graceful in its architectural style. Wellington is buried here alongside Nelson, and there are memorials to a number of distinguished contributors to the arts including Henry Moore, Edwin Lutyens, Sir Arthur Sullivan and William Blake. The Chapel of the Order of the British Empire is also here, as is the Treasury.

WESTMINSTER CATHEDRAL

FOR THE AVERAGE explorer of English cathedrals and churches, to enter John Francis Bentley's Byzantine basilican Westminster Cathedral is to enter a new world. The sense of 'mystical space' together with the lofty dark domes, marble and mosaics is more familiar to the traveller in Ravenna or Istanbul. Cardinal Vaughan, whose energy made possible the construction of this remarkable building, was clear that he did not want Gothic; his intention had been that the cathedral should be a Roman style basilica, and so Bentley's Byzantine solution was initially a surprise even to him.

The cathedral is conceived of as a single whole and the nave is both the highest and broadest in the country, giving an unimpeded view of the high altar, which stands beneath a majestic baldachino of Verona marble. There are transepts, but these are cleverly caught up architecturally into the basilical space. Building began in 1895 and the cathedral was consecrated in 1910. The nave consists of three square bays crowned with domes; this structure is supported cleverly by a series of subsidiary side arches. The nave piers are covered in dark green marble from Thessaly in northern Greece which was used centuries ago for the decoration of Hagia Sophia in Constantinople (Istanbul).

The sanctuary is marked off from the nave space by the great 30-foot-high hanging rood crucifix by Christian Symons. The splendid nave piers are also used for the magnificent Stations of the Cross by Eric Gill, which stand among the sculptor's finest works. The sense of journey often experienced when moving from nave to sanctuary in a Gothic

church is not lost, but is instead replaced by a similar journey made via the side chapels; it is a journey from birth to death, beginning at the baptistry in the south-west corner, as one enters, and ending with the Chapel of the Holy Souls, as one leaves the building from its north-west corner. Included among the other chapels is a shrine to St John Southworth, a Reformation martyr, in the chapel of St George and the English Martyrs. This chapel also contains a fine bas-relief by Eric Gill.

The front of Westminster Cathedral with the piazza created in the 1960s

Mosaic tympanum over the west door

SOUTHWARK CATHEDRAL

HIDDEN BETWEEN LONDON Bridge, extensive railway arches and the remains of Thameside wharves, Southwark Cathedral is a rarely discovered architectural gem. There has probably been a church here for over a thousand years, the original having been built over a Roman villa (Southwark was a suburb of Londinium). In the mid-ninth century St Swithun, Bishop of Winchester, within whose diocese it lay, set up a college of priests, and there are still some ruins of a palace of the bishops of Winchester nearby. In Edward the Confessor's time a monastery was established here.

The origins of the present church lie in the foundation of a priory of Augustinian canons set up to serve the new church of St Mary Overie (over the river) in the year 1106; the same canons set up St Thomas' Hospital. Very few traces of this original Norman work survive, due to a serious fire in 1212. The church was rebuilt between 1220 and 1273; the fine Early English work in the quire, retro-quire and quire aisles dates from this period. Also completed then were the lower parts of the tower and the western bays of the nave. In 1283 construction resumed and the main structure, including the nave and transepts, was finished by the

The nave looking west from the choir

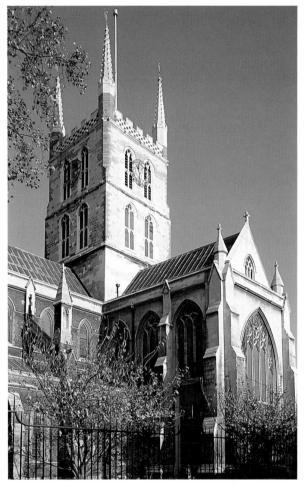

Southwark Cathedral from the south-west

mid-fourteenth century. Disaster struck again in the 1390s with another fire, but by 1420 the rebuilding was complete; this included the rest of the tower and the rebuilding of the south transept.

In 1469, the nave roof collapsed leading to further rebuilding. The magnificent Perpendicular screen between the high altar and the retro-quire was given by Richard Fox, the then Bishop of Winchester, in 1520. After the Reformation, the priory having been dissolved, the church became the parish church of St Saviour. John Harvard was baptised here in 1607 and is commemorated in the Harvard Chapel, and Lancelot Andrewes, the saintly bishop of Winchester, is buried in the cathedral. In 1890 the foundation stone was laid of the present Victorian Gothic nave. With the carving out of the diocese of Southwark from Winchester, the church became a cathedral in 1905. The new chapter house was opened by Her Majesty the Queen in 1988.

WESTMINSTER ABBEY

IT IS DIFFICULT to exaggerate the significance of Westminster Abbey with regard to its place in national life. Not only was it the burial place of kings, but also it remains the place where the monarch is crowned, the church for so many poignant national occasions, and the home of memorials of so many who have contributed to the political, scientific and cultural life of the nation. A community of Benedictine monks was first settled here by St Dunstan around 960, but the abbey and collegiate church of Westminster owes much to the refoundation by Edward the Confessor, even though none of his church is now visible above the ground. St Edward (as he later became) rebuilt the abbey in Romanesque style, completing it in 1065. He

himself died a few weeks later; his shrine is still at the heart of the abbey.

The church as we now know it is largely the work of King Henry III who began the demolition of the eastern part of the Norman church in 1245 and set about rebuilding in the Early English style. That style is clearly visible in the chancel and the grand plan for the new church was never abandoned despite the extended period of its rebuilding. The most familiar external views of the abbey are from Parliament Square and these show very clearly the strong French influence. It is the most French in style of all English Gothic churches with its radiating chapels around the apse and its ambulatory. Even Henry Yevele, the mason

The quire looking towards the shrine of Edward the Confessor

pavement around the shrine is thirteenth-century patterned Cosmati work, and of similar design to the pavement in the presbytery. The shrine itself still includes the recesses where the sick knelt, hoping for a cure through the relics of the saint. The Coronation Chair of 1301 is nearby; the Stone of Scone which was set beneath the seat is now once again in Scotland, in Edinburgh Castle. Around the shrine runs the ambulatory with its radiating chapels of St John the Baptist, St Paul, St Nicholas and St Edmund and St Thomas.

Beyond the chancel and shrine opens up the dazzling fan-vaulting of the Henry VII Chapel; this late Perpendicular masterpiece was completed in 1509. The pendant-like vaulting is perhaps the most stunning of its type. The cloisters were rebuilt after a great fire in 1298, although the eastern walk includes some work from earlier in the thirteenth century; the little cloister with its surrounding houses stands on the site of the monastic infirmary. The splendid chapter house stands on the east side of the east cloister. Dean's Yard was originally partly covered by monastic buildings and the chapter office and school houses incorporate much of the fourteenth century guest house and cellarers' quarters. Far more of the monastic complex has survived here because of the close links between the abbey and the state.

One cannot begin to catalogue the tombs and memorials which find their place in this remarkable building. Alongside kings stand memorials to countless literary figures in Poet's Corner; Isaac Newton and other great scientists are remembered in the nave, and then politicians and soldiers complete the catalogue of the makers of English history.

who built the nave (and who also rebuilt the nave of Canterbury Cathedral in its majestic Perpendicular style) continued the plan laid out a hundred years before, when he completed the western part of the nave beginning in 1375. The unusual height of the nave vaulting (102 feet) is a further sign of the French influence.

The niches above the great west door were recently filled with effigies of ten twentieth-century martyrs, including the Polish monk Maximilian Kolbe. The twin towers on this front are a late addition, designed by Christopher Wren, modified by Nicholas Hawksmoor and completed by his successor as architect, John James. The western nave was the last part of the mediaeval building to be completed in 1403. Immediately inside the west door are the Grave of the Unknown Warrior, placed there after World War I, and a memorial to Sir Winston Churchill.

One moves from the nave into the quire through a screen to find oneself among stalls completed in 1848. The quire opens out into the crossing and the whole of this eastern arm, including the chapter house, was complete by 1259. The chancel is divided by the reredos into the presbytery and the Chapel, which encloses the shrine of Edward the Confessor. The

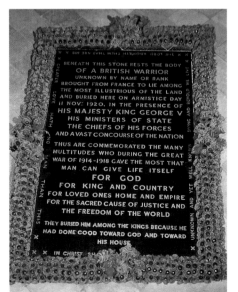

The Grave of the Unknown Warrior

ROCHESTER CATHEDRAL

transepts (including in the north transept some of the best Gothic work in the cathedral) were built in the mid-to late thirteenth century.

The original central tower and spire, completed in 1345, were the work of Bishop Hamo de Hythe; both were remodelled in the nineteenth century and the present spire was completed in 1904. Bishop de Hythe was also responsible for the splendid chapter room doorway, a fine example of the Decorated style. The fifteenth century saw the addition of the great west window, placed in the centre of the Romanesque façade. During the Reformation period, Rochester produced two martyrs, one from either side of the divide. Bishop John Fisher became a martyr for the Catholic cause when he was beheaded by King Henry VIII in 1535. Nineteen years later, Bishop Nicholas Ridley was burned during the reign of Mary Tudor and became a martyr to the Protestant cause. Ridley is commemorated by a figure in the nineteenth-century quire screen.

AFTER CANTERBURY, ROCHESTER is effectively the oldest diocese in England, Augustine having sent one of his fellow monks there to be the first bishop in 604. The mortal remains of Paulinus, the great missionary to Northumbria, are still in this cathedral. Nothing is visible of the Saxon cathedral, and it is the church begun by the Norman bishop, Gundulf, in 1077 of which the earliest remains are visible. Gundulf founded a Benedictine community and set to work on constructing a new Romanesque church. Parts of his cathedral are still visible in the nave arcading, in the western part of the crypt and in his tower on the north side of the cathedral. The magnificent Romanesque western façade belongs to the later period of building around 1160. The remains of the monastic cloister and chapter house are from the period 1115–37.

The earliest Gothic work, begun around 1180, can be traced in the enlarged quire, which was completed with its perfect Early English vault in 1227. During this period a square ended presbytery was added, without aisles or ambulatory. The broad quire transepts were also built at this time and work also continued westwards into the nave, with the complete rebuilding of the first two bays. The north and south nave

The Romanesque western door arch and tympanum

AYLESFORD PRIORY

THE CARMELITE FRIARS first came to Aylesford in 1242 when Richard de Grey gave land for a priory. The first church was dedicated in 1248, and around 1280 the Pilgrims' Hall, a guest house was built. At the beginning of the fourteenth century, following generous endowments, rebuilding began. The church was begun in 1348 and completed in 1417. After the Reformation the priory eventually fell into the hands of Sir John Sedley who converted it into a country house. During the 1930s the then owner restored much of the complex to its mediaeval monastic style.

Carmelite friars returned to Aylesford Priory in 1949. The restored refectory became the chapel and eventually the buildings were transformed. The Pilgrims' Hall has reverted to its original use and, in 1965, Adrian Gilbert Scott's new shrine for the remains of St Simon Stock (and associated chapels) were consecrated. Also within the grounds is a fine seventeenth-century thatched tithe barn which now acts as a tea-room and shop. The priory is a popular centre of pilgrimage and is very much a place for ecumenical encounter.

Aylesford Priory: the courtyard

The priory and the River Medway

ARUNDEL CATHEDRAL

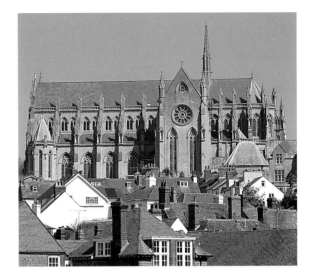

AS WITH THE Roman Catholic cathedral in Norwich, so in Arundel the building was made possible through the generosity of the 15th duke of Norfolk. It is a magnificent example of nineteenth-century Gothic revival in the French style of around 1400. The architect was Joseph Hansom, who designed Birmingham Town Hall and the Hansom Cab.

The cathedral from the south

Arundel Cathedral exudes a sense of height, both from exterior and interior elevations. It has an aisled nave of six bays and is cruciform in plan with an apsidal sanctuary, again following the style of French Gothic. In the nave the arcades with their slender columns and pointed arches add to the sense of height. In the north transept are the remains of St Philip Howard, Earl of Arundel, who was martyred in 1595 during the reign of Queen Elizabeth I. There is a noble western gallery housing the organ and beyond that a fine rose window.

Detail above the great west door: the rose window

CANTERBURY CATHEDRAL

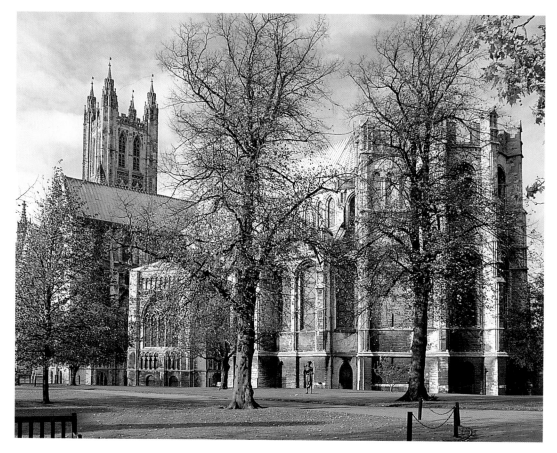

CANTERBURY IS INCOMPARABLE, for it is both the shrine to the birth of English Christianity and also the beating heart of the Anglican Communion. It was Thomas Becket's murder in 1170 within the cathedral by four knights of the court of Henry II that would make Canterbury, along with Compostela, one of the holiest shrines of mediaeval Europe. But Canterbury's history goes back well beyond Becket's martyrdom. For it was to the court of King Ethelbert of Kent that Pope Gregory sent Augustine in AD 597. Augustine came to a city where there were already Christian churches and even the cathedral appears to have been built on the foundation of an earlier church. Something of this continuity was further pressed home when the nave floor was re-paved in 1993, and the foundations of the Saxon cathedral were discovered.

Canterbury sits regally in low lying land. Its two western towers and the majestic Bell Harry tower at its centre lift the heart. The cathedral precincts are entered through the Christ Church Gate beneath the new sculpture of Christ by Klaus Ringwald. The Perpendicular west front was built in the 1420s by

Thomas Mapilton, as was the south-west tower, but the north-west tower, a copy of Mapilton's work, was built in the 1820s when the original Norman tower at last began to crumble.

Entering Henry Yevele's breathtaking late-fourteenth century Perpendicular nave is a truly inspiring experience. It is a perfectly patterned format of Perpendicular piers of great height. The canopied vaulting is spectacular as indeed is the sheer sense of space. To the north of the crossing is the 'Martyrdom', the site of Becket's untimely death. The crossing itself is a place of high architectural drama. Well worn steps lead up to the pulpitum screen and high above is the dazzling fan-vaulting of the Bell Harry tower.

The broad quire lies behind the pulpitum, and at the eastern end, behind the high altar, is the thirteenth-century Purbeck 'Chair of St Augustine'. The chair was moved there from the Corona Chapel in July 1977. It reminds pilgrims, and all who come, of the focal role of the Archbishop of Canterbury, not only in the Church

The Bell Harry tower and the east end, from the south-east

of England but in the world-wide Anglican Communion.

The quire at Canterbury is an unusual piece of very early Gothic; it is almost possible to feel the transition taking place between Romanesque and incipient Gothic. Behind the high altar is the Trinity Chapel, the ultimate destination of mediaeval pilgrims; it was to here that the relics of Becket were translated in the early thirteenth century and placed in the heart of a magnificent shrine. The building of the quire began almost immediately after Becket's martyrdom. The builder was William of Sens, who had been brought directly from his work on the new cathedral at Sens in France. In the 1540s the agents of Henry VIII dismantled the shrine and crumbled it brutally beyond any possibility of reconstruction. At the far east end of the cathedral, beyond the Trinity Chapel, lies the Corona Chapel, now dedicated to the memory of twentieth-century martyrs.

Canterbury may be regarded as a great monastic church. Augustine, like his patron Pope Gregory the Great was a monk, and Canterbury grew to be a great Benedictine foundation with over 100 monks. A walk through the precincts to the north of the cathedral will give a fairly clear picture of the old monastic buildings. The dark

Henry Yevele's Perpendicular nave

Fan-vaulting beneath the Bell Harry tower

entry is surmounted by a canon's house and to the west is the cloister around which the monastic buildings, including the refectory and the dormitories, would have been clustered. The chapter house survives, and immediately beneath the east end of the cathedral is the vast crypt including the Black Prince's chantry chapel and in the centre the Lady Chapel of the crypt.

From the outside of the cathedral it is possible to sense the development of the building, with fragments of Romanesque surviving in the east which then grow into early Gothic. The Bell Harry tower and the nave complete the picture with the later Perpendicular work. The close proximity of St Augustine's Abbey and of the King's School, together with the cathedral's monastic ruins, are symbolic of the historic and central part that Canterbury has played in the development of Christianity in England.

BATTLE ABBEY

Battle Abbey: the great mediaeval gatehouse

There are virtually no signs of the abbey church now above ground, but parts of the former monastery – converted and modernised by Sir Anthony Browne into a country residence in the 1530s and then, in the twentieth century, into a girls' public school – can still be seen. The building of the abbey began around 1070 and was finished around two decades later. It was a Benedictine foundation and it was further extended and added to in the twelfth century and again later. A re-fashioned east end with chevet chapels was built onto the church in the late thirteenth century, after the style of Westminster Abbey. The most significant remains still visible are those of the great gatehouse, the western range (the part of the building that was converted), the eastern range with the reredorter and associated rooms, and finally the guest range. The gatehouse is one of the finest examples of a monastic gatehouse in England. In its present form it dates from 1338 and many of the mediaeval chambers within it remain. The western range was rebuilt in the thirteenth century and it includes the Great Hall, which can be viewed only in the school holidays.

THE SIGNIFICANCE FOR English history of the Battle of Hastings and the subsequent Norman Conquest can hardly be exaggerated. The cultural implications were enormous, not least in the development of ecclesiastical architecture. It appears that Battle Abbey was built on this site as a penance imposed by the Papal authorities in 1070 for the bloodshed caused by the Norman invasion. Tradition has it that the high altar of the abbey church was placed at the point where King Harold died in the heat of battle.

The outline of the cloister is still visible, now marked with gravel paths. The most splendid survival in the eastern range is the loftily vaulted novices' chamber; signs of the Early English work are clear in the lancets at the southern end of this range. The guest range was extensively rebuilt after the Reformation by Sir Anthony Browne and the two western corner towers are all that remain from this period of rebuilding.

GUILDFORD CATHEDRAL

Exterior of the cathedral from the south-east

THE ONLY NEW cathedral to be built in the province of Canterbury during the twentieth century commands a magnificent site to the north-west of Guildford. The ground crowning Stag Hill was given by the earl of Onslow as a site for the cathedral of the diocese, which was formed out of part of Winchester diocese in 1927. Building on the site began in 1936, was halted by the outbreak of war three years later, and was resumed in 1952. It was finally consecrated in 1961.

The cathedral, built of modern materials, is clad on the outside mainly by brick with some Clipsham stone, and on the inside with plaster and Doulting stone from Somerset. The style is modernised Gothic with soaring pointed arches, giving the fine interior a sense of dignified austerity. Dedicated to the Holy Spirit, the nave arches, reaching upward, witness to the mystery of God, as intended by Sir Edward Maufe, the architect. The cathedral is of a cruciform plan with narrow transepts, and a narthex, the two arms of which extend at the west front.

The nave of seven bays has a floor of travertine stone with its arches clad in Doulting stone and plaster. The vistas are completely open, with one's eyes being carried directly to the great golden dorsal curtain which is 45 feet high and is surmounted by the rose window by Moira Forsyth. The window depicts the dove descending, picking up the theme of the Holy Spirit, to whom the cathedral is dedicated. At the western end of the south aisle is the baptistry with a font made also of travertine stone. The organ fills the north transept, and beyond the high altar is the Lady Chapel. There is also a regimental chapel and a modern chapter house.

The exterior mass of the cathedral powerfully dominates Stag Hill, culminating in the strong central tower, which is crowned with a golden angel facing in the direction of the prevailing wind. The building is now flanked by the University of Surrey, creating a link with the city and bringing together the civic, the intellectual and the spiritual life of Guildford.

The austere beauty of the cathedral interior

CHICHESTER CATHEDRAL

St Wilfrid was one of the most determined of the early missionaries in Anglo-Saxon England. His determination, however, also provoked opposition, and it was exile from Northumbria that brought Wilfrid to the southern Saxons. He set up a cathedral in Selsey in 681 and there it remained for four hundred years. Following their conquest in 1066, the Normans carried out their consistent policy and moved the cathedral to the former Roman town now known as Chichester. This took place in 1075, and construction began very soon after.

It was Bishop Luffa who ensured that the main structure of the cathedral as we now see it came to be. By 1123, the nave, transepts, choir and eastern chapels were largely complete. The Romanesque building was formally dedicated in 1108. In 1187, a fire extensively damaged the east end of the building and the apse was replaced with a two bay retro-choir in the Transitional style. The three eastern bays of the Lady Chapel were added around 1300 in the Decorated style, with vaulting. The episcopate of Richard of Wych (St Richard of Chichester) from 1245–53 was significant because of his pastoral zeal; following his canonisation a shrine was eventually set up in the retro-choir. Destroyed at the Reformation, the site has now regained its significance as a destination for pilgrims, and nearby are two remarkable Romanesque stone carved panels dating from around 1125. Conflict during the Civil War also wreaked havoc, with the Deanery and the Chancellor's House being

The cathedral from the south-west

destroyed, along with fittings and books. The fifteenth century left its mark upon the cathedral with the construction of the delightful cloisters in Perpendicular style – Chichester was never a monastic cathedral. In 1436 the great detached bell tower was built to the north of the west front and in 1475 Bishop John Arundel added the fine stone pulpitum and choir screen; this was removed in the nineteenth century but happily restored in memory of Bishop George Bell in 1961. This restoration was the initiative of Walter Hussey who, as Dean, commissioned work by some fine twentieth-century artists. Examples include John Piper's striking tapestry behind the high altar (1966) and Graham Sutherland's painting *Noli me Tangere*.

Detail of a Romanesque carved stone panel depicting the raising of Lazarus

PORTSMOUTH CATHEDRAL

THE NAVAL TRADITION of the city of Portsmouth has coloured this delightful cathedral. Its tower and lantern have long been signals of homecoming to seamen over the centuries. Since 1984 the grave of an unknown sailor from the Mary Rose (wrecked off Portsmouth in 1545) has added a further poignant maritime focus, this time inside the cathedral, in the Navy Aisle. The cathedral began as the parish church of St Thomas of Canterbury, and became a cathedral in 1927, with the creation of the new diocese of Portsmouth.

The east end is the earliest part of the building, now the chapel of St Thomas, with a focus in the splendid hanging pyx by Hector Miller. The chancel was completed in the Transitional style in 1185 – the dedication to Thomas Becket was topical since he had been martyred in Canterbury Cathedral in 1170. The original mediaeval church continued westward to form a cruciform building with a tower at its west end.

The core of this building is still clearly seen in the transepts (now the Lady Chapel and the Martyr Chapel) and in the shape of the central part of the quire (the original nave).

The west front and tower, from the south-west

During the Civil War the church was bombarded from Gosport by Parliamentary troops and severe damage was sustained. The nave and tower were left ruinous and this led to the deterioration of the fine mediaeval wall-painting, some of which is still preserved in the north transept. By 1691, the nave and tower were rebuilt in the restrained elegance of the William and Mary Classical style. Already Gothic and Classical stood side by side.

The foundation of the new diocese of Portsmouth brought another architectural style into play. Sir Charles Nicholson added tower transepts and the beginnings of a nave in Rhenish Romanesque. By 1939 these plans had been completed as far as the third bay of the nave. The completion of the cathedral had to wait until 1991. Michael Drury's final bay and west work reflected Nicholson's vision. Included are a Byzantine-style font beneath the tower and the new bronze west doors, representing the tree of life, which were designed by Bryan Kneale and were dedicated in 1998. The original Golden Barque weather vane is now within the cathedral itself.

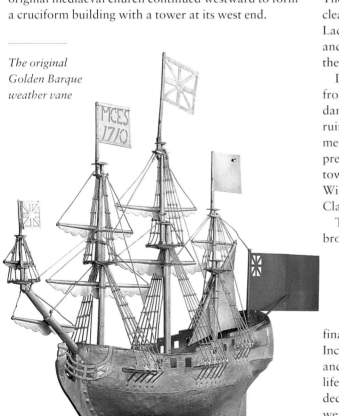

The original Golden Barque weather vane

WINCHESTER CATHEDRAL

THE BEGINNINGS OF Winchester Cathedral lie back in the seventh-century missions to England when St Birinus baptised King Cynegils of the West Saxons in the year 635. In 643 Cenwalh built a minster at Winchester and Bishop Haeddi transferred his see there around three decades later, establishing the minster as his cathedral. Winchester thus became a royal and ecclesiastical centre – mortuary chests with the bones of these kings and queens are still in the possession of the cathedral; Alfred the Great, king of Wessex, was buried in the minster in 899. In the 960s Bishop Ethelwold re-founded the cathedral as a Benedictine priory, dedicated to St Swithun, the ninth-century saint. The replacement of the Saxon bishop Stigand with Walkelin, a Norman, in 1070 marks the beginnings of the present cathedral. Walkelin began building in 1079 and the first part of the building was dedicated in 1093. When the nave was completed, Winchester became the longest cathedral in England at an extraordinary length of 535 feet. Most of Walkelin's cathedral has been rebuilt and above ground only the transepts give us an idea of the appearance of his church.

The modest but noble Perpendicular work on the west front gives way to the magnificent nave, also Perpendicular in style. The present nave is not as long as its Romanesque predecessor, but its majesty contributes to making Winchester still the longest cathedral in England at a total length of 556 feet. The remodelling of the nave was begun by Bishop William Edington in the mid-fourteenth century and completed by the famous Bishop William of Wykeham, who was the founder of both New College, Oxford, and Winchester College. The nave's height and vaulting give it a splendid dignity. The two transepts are the only remaining examples of Romanesque work above ground (the crypt also survives in Romanesque style).

More Perpendicular arcading can be found in the nineteenth-century choir screen, while the choir itself is set beneath the enormous arches of the central tower. Within the choir are very fine choir stalls with misericords, dating from around 1308, which are

(There are also two fine chantries in the nave to William of Edington and William Wykeham.) The chantry chapels in Winchester are celebrated examples of such chapels which were built so that daily masses could be said by the monks for the bishops commemorated within them. William Waynflete stands alongside William of Wykeham as a great founder and benefactor in English education; he was Provost of Eton and founded Magdalen College, Oxford. Stephen Gardiner was the last bishop of Winchester to pay allegiance to the Pope, surviving the Reformations of both Henry VIII and Edward VI before dying during the reign of Mary Tudor.

Winchester Cathedral has associations with the writers Izaak Walton and Jane Austen, both of whom are buried here. There are a also number of important contemporary art commissions, including Antony Gormley's sculpture *Sound II* in the crypt and Peter Eugene Ball's *Christus* in the north transept. In the retro-choir, and on the screen separating the feretory from the shrine, are a number of modern icons, in the Byzantine style, by Sergei Fedorov. Winchester, following the example of Walter Hussey in Chichester, has re-established the tradition of the Church as a patron of the arts.

The memorial to St Swithun believed to be the work of William Lyngwode, a Norfolk carpenter. The wooden vaulting of the presbytery is built to mirror the stone vaulting of the nave. At the eastern end of the presbytery, between the choir and the retro-choir, is the remarkable Great Screen which dates from the late fifteenth century, with its numerous niches containing a series of stone figures. The original figures were broken up at the Reformation, but many have since been recovered and are now displayed in the triforium gallery; the present figures date from the late nineteenth century.

The retro-choir was opened up to its present enormous size around 1200 in the Early English style to house the shrine with the remains of St Swithun; this work was begun by Bishop Godfrey de Lucy, whose austere tomb of Purbeck marble stands within this retro-choir. St Swithun's relics were translated to their final resting place near to the present memorial in 1476, but in 1538, at the Dissolution, the shrine was destroyed and the location of Swithun's bones is unknown. The Lady Chapel, which was part of this, was altered and re-vaulted around 1500. Surrounding the retro-choir are magnificent chantry chapels to Cardinal Henry Beaufort and Bishops William Waynflete, Richard Fox and Stephen Gardiner.

The nave, looking east

THE SOUTH WEST

THE ANCIENT kingdom of Kernow (Cornwall) contains some unusual roots for Christianity in England. The profusion of local saints and the relatively late survival of Celtic patterns (the Cornish were the last to accept the canons of the Synod of Whitby) still flavour the culture of the far South West. Although Truro Cathedral is relatively modern, it is alone amongst English cathedrals in being set cheek-by-jowl with other buildings in the heart of the city, rather after the French pattern.

In Devon, equally distinctive are Exeter Cathedral's twin Norman towers at the crossing; the dramatic Gothic scissor arches in Wells Cathedral in Somerset are unique. There are a number of other gems not to be missed: Salisbury with its perfect exterior massing is the most consistently conceived mediaeval cathedral in England. Bath Abbey's fan vaulting represents the climax of the Perpendicular style. Sherborne Abbey and Wimborne Minster are amongst a small number of 'great churches' within England. Bristol brings together stunning Romanesque in its chapter house with fine Gothic Revival in its nave. Buckfast Abbey is twentieth century mediaeval rebuilt by the monks, and Clifton Roman Catholic Cathedral represents a unique attempt to build a cathedral respecting the principles of the twentieth century liturgical revival.

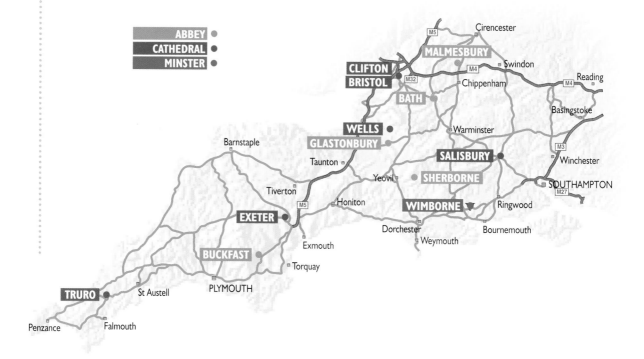

MALMESBURY ABBEY

A SEVENTH-CENTURY monk, later canonised as St Aldhelm, founded the Benedictine abbey at Malmesbury. The Romanesque nave survives as a parish church with its pointed transitional arcades and rounded Norman triforium. The east wall stands where the screen at the crossing once stood. Outside, the arch into the north transept still survives. Also externally, the Romanesque blind arcading still points to the majesty of the building. The Norman carvings above the south porch are particularly fine.

Malmesbury Abbey from the south

Romanesque detail around the south porch

One of the curious features of the abbey is the box-like structure at triforium level on the south side of the nave; it is not certain whether it was there as an observation post or as a place of penance. Malmesbury has associations with two significant figures from the past – the tomb commemorating King Athelstan (king of England from 925–939) is at the eastern end of the north aisle, and William of Malmesbury, arguably the greatest English historian between Bede and Gibbon, spent nearly his whole life in the monastery.

CLIFTON CATHEDRAL

Clifton Cathedral with its combined flèche and bell tower

THE MODERN ROMAN Catholic Cathedral of St Peter and St Paul at Clifton in Bristol replaced the pro-cathedral dedicated to the Apostles which opened in 1848. The new cathedral has benefited from the insights of the contemporary liturgical movement. Hence the altar effectively stands at the focus of a quadrant, giving good sight lines for all when mass is celebrated.

Externally, there is a striking flèche containing a cross and two bells. The construction is of shuttered concrete and the simplicity of the main structure allows the internal furnishings to speak eloquently. The font is by Simon Verity and is of Portland Stone with a Spangled Purbeck bowl; there is some fine lettering around the rim. The stations of the cross, the ambo and lectern, all of which include some interesting modern relief work, are by William Mitchell. The altar is square and of Portland Stone, reflecting the overall effect of the interior of the cathedral, which is one of striking simplicity.

BRISTOL CATHEDRAL

BRISTOL CATHEDRAL IS set on College Green at the centre of the modern city. It goes back to an initiative by Robert Fitzhardinge, who brought six Augustinian monks to establish the first abbey here in 1140. The first church, in Romanesque style, was probably completed by 1165. The chapter house, which leads off the eastern cloister walk, survives from that period, and is a particularly notable piece of Romanesque architecture. In 1220 the Elder Lady Chapel (the older of the two Lady chapels) was built in the new Gothic style. It is situated off the north transept, and it has exquisite carvings of foliage, beasts and human faces.

Soon after the completion of this chapel, the monks began to make plans for the rebuilding of the Romanesque church in the prevailing Gothic style. They began with the eastern Lady Chapel and then continued westward into the choir. A notable feature of this work is that the roofs of the Choir aisles are the same height as those of the Choir itself, thus forming a 'hall church'. The eastern Lady Chapel was subsequently adorned with some fine carving, including the arms of the earls of Berkeley, descendants of the Fitzhardinges. The choir is notable for the beautiful pattern made by the lierne ribs of the vaulting, among the earliest such vaults in England. The choir stalls contain some notable wood carving from those given by Abbot Elyot in about 1520 and they include some fine misericords.

The cathedral from the south-west

The tower and transepts were refashioned in the period 1460–80, and the vaulting of the transepts and the crossing is particularly fine. When the abbey was closed by King Henry VIII in 1539 the monks had just embarked on a scheme to rebuild the nave in the Gothic style, the Romanesque nave having already been demolished in preparation for this. The cathedral remained without a nave until 1867, when G. E. Street began to build on the foundations of the original pillars. J. L. Pearson, who designed Truro Cathedral, subsequently added the present high altar reredos and the choir screen. The western towers were completed in 1888, after Street's death.

BATH ABBEY

Bath's Christian roots go back to the Roman origins of the town, but the first certain recorded date is of 757 where the monastery of St Peter in Bath is mentioned, and in time a Benedictine community was established. It was here in 973 that Edgar was crowned the first king of all England, commemorated by Queen Elizabeth II's visit in 1973. In 1090 Bishop John de Villula of Wells moved his seat to Bath and began building a great Romanesque cathedral and abbey buildings. The cathedral, half as long again as the present abbey, may have been one of the longest churches in England. It was completed around 1170 and some fragments of the stone of this abbey church can be seen in Bath Abbey Heritage Vaults Museum. The only real sign of this earlier building visible in the present abbey is a round-headed arch in the east wall of the so-called Norman Chapel. In 1244 the diocese transferred back to Wells and Bath's influence waned.

The west front of the abbey

It was in 1499, with the initiative

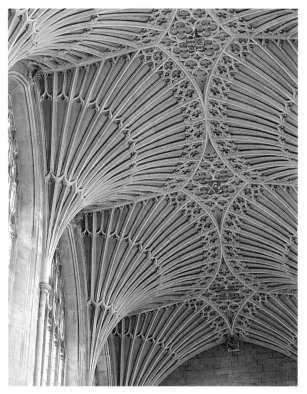

The remarkable fan-vaulting within the abbey

of Bishop Oliver King, that Bath Abbey moved back into prominence. King began the present church which was the last major Perpendicular building in England and the apotheosis of the Perpendicular style. This can be appreciated in the nobility of the west front with its fine carvings, including Oliver King's rebus of the olive tree and the crown, and his splendid vision of ascending angels. Inside the building, apart from the sense of height, the great triumph is the glorious fan-vaulting of local Bath stone. This effusion of Perpendicular extravagance is continued in the chantry chapel, of Prior William Bird, who died in 1525. Perhaps the most splendid feature of the two small transepts is the slender Jesse window in the south transept which extends from the tomb of Sir William Waller to the vaulting above.

Bath is justly famous for its memorials and plaques. In the south nave aisle is the burial place of Beau Nash who helped establish the reputation of the city as a spa in the eighteenth century. In 1997, the Chapel of St Alphege was consecrated, commemorating Bath's most celebrated abbot, who became Archbishop of Canterbury and was martyred in the early part of the eleventh century.

SALISBURY CATHEDRAL

The spire and east end from the north-east

Like an intricate casket on a carpet of mown grass – this is but one description of the remarkable integrity of Salisbury Cathedral. This integrity and proportion, which we see uniquely in Salisbury amongst the mediaeval English cathedrals, owes its origins to the initiative of Bishop Richard le Poore. In 1217, he petitioned the Pope for leave to remove his cathedral to a new site. The earlier cathedral had been built in Romanesque style by the Norman bishop Osmund. This cathedral had been at Old Sarum, and it was in this place, through the work of St Osmund, that the statutes of the cathedral were formulated and perhaps even during this period that the interest in liturgy, which gave birth to the 'Sarum Rite' began. As a site, however, Old Sarum was unsatisfactory – it was short of water and extremely exposed.

The new cathedral was begun in 1220 at a point where two rivers find their confluence with the Avon. The unity of its Early English architecture owes all to the building being completed within fifty years. The masons started in the east with the Chapel of the Holy Trinity and All Saints; on its completion in 1225 it became the new site of the tomb of St Osmund, moved here from Old Sarum. Despite Richard le Poore's move to Durham, the cathedral was still finished to the original design. The Trinity Chapel is the most daring and original part of the cathedral with its slender pillars of Purbeck marble and very narrow side aisles. The chapel was transfigured in 1980 with the addition of the magnificent Prisoners of Conscience window by Gabriel Loire of Chartres. The thirteenth-century colouring, with deep blues, adds an aura of mystery to

the whole cathedral with its wide and open vistas from west to east.

The building of the cathedral continued eastwards and the cloisters too were constructed in the period 1240–70. The cloisters were built partly to form a passage to the chapter house – Salisbury was never a monastic foundation. The chapter house was completed between 1263 and 1284 and is a superb example of the Geometrical Decorated style, similar to that at Westminster Abbey, with a roof fanning out from a single central pillar. The cathedral is built throughout from Jurassic limestone from Chilmark to the west of Salisbury, while the pillars are of Purbeck marble from Worth Matravers in Dorset. One of the merits of Salisbury Cathedral is the clarity and simplicity of its design. It is among the larger English cathedrals and its most majestic and famous feature is, of course, its spire. It is the tallest spire in England, reaching a height of 404 feet. The construction of the spire is remarkable, being based upon an interior wooden scaffolding which remains to this day. The great load (6,400 tons) is borne by the four main central piers, supported by a series of internal stone buttresses, built into the thickness of the clerestory walls to help take the strain. Strainer arches were added in the fourteenth century at the entrance to the choir transepts to supplement the other arches into the transept and to avoid the great piers collapsing inwards.

The bishop and chapter added a library over the eastern cloister in 1445. Within the library is a fine collection of mediaeval manuscripts, including a Gallican Psalter of the tenth century. Most famous of all is its copy of the Magna Carta, one of four copies, another of which is in the library at Lincoln Cathedral. Originally this building was twice its present length and included the Chancellor's Lecture Room. The restoration of Salisbury Cathedral by James Wyatt from 1789–92 has been much criticised, mainly because of what he removed, including the high altar, the thirteenth-century choir screen, and the detached bell tower. He also took out the remaining thirteenth-century glass from the windows and removed two fifteenth-century chantry chapels; even so the removal of these chapels restored the original plan of the cathedral. Thirty years later the high altar was replaced and the arrangement of the sanctuary reverted to the earlier plan.

Salisbury stands within the largest open close in England with splendid housing all around. Elizabeth Frink's *Walking Madonna* adds an interesting feature to the north-west corner of the Close, as the visitor approaches from the city gate. The city itself was begun at the same time as the cathedral and is the earliest example in England of a city built upon a planned 'grid' of streets.

WELLS CATHEDRAL

A GLIMPSE OF the elaborate and highly sculptured west front, the chapter house stairs and the great scissor arches at the crossing is more than sufficient reason to make a special pilgrimage to Wells. That, combined with the springs that feed the moat of the Bishop's Palace and give the city its name, offer something unparalleled in any English cathedral. The first church on this site was built by Aldhelm in 705; in 909 the diocese was founded and Aldhelm's church became the cathedral. In 1088 it was rebuilt by Bishop Robert of Lewes, but not until 1244 did the Pope decree the diocese be named Bath and Wells, and the church became a cathedral once more.

The cathedral was the first to be built in English Gothic and much of the building is in Decorated style. The aisled nave dates from 1239. The view of the crossing is dominated by William Joy's scissor arches (1378), designed to bear the weight of the tower which was beginning to crumble under its own weight.

The west front with its countless niches

The upper stage of the tower is Perpendicular in style, dating from around 1439. The scissor arches exude both strength and grace. Beyond the pulpitum screen is the earliest part of the cathedral, which was begun around 1179. In 1320 the quire was extended eastwards and eventually made to connect with the octagonal Lady Chapel which had earlier been a quite separate building. There are fine stalls with misericords dating from the same period. There is good mediaeval glass in both the east window and in the windows of the quire aisles.

In the south transept is the Saxon font, the only surviving feature of the earlier church. To the east of the north transept, are the stunning chapter house stairs which lead eventually to the Chain Gate and Vicars' Hall. Wells has always been governed by a dean and canons and in early days served by the Vicars' Choral. The Vicars' Choral lived in Vicars' Close and met in Vicars' Hall. Although Wells was never a monastic foundation, it does have a particularly beautiful mediaeval cloister which, in its present form, dates back to the fifteenth century.

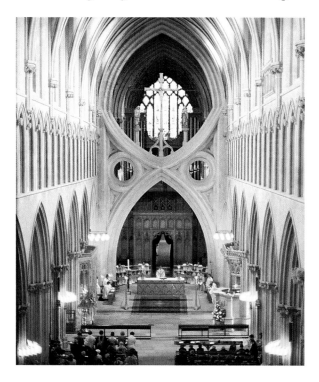

Wells' unique scissor arches

SHERBORNE ABBEY

SHERBORNE ABBEY'S HISTORY begins with the establishment of the diocese with Aldhelm, Abbot of Malmesbury, as its first bishop in AD 705. The Saxon building became both an abbey church and a cathedral in 998, with the introduction of a community of Benedictine monks by Bishop Wulfsin. The see lasted for almost four hundred years. In 1058 Ramsbury was joined with Sherborne but in 1075, following the Norman Conquest, the diocese was given a new centre at Old Sarum.

Saxon stonework is still visible in the abbey, and the doorway at the west end of the north aisle is from this period. The Norman rebuilding probably began in the mid-twelfth century and elements of this can be seen in the arches at the crossing and in the walls of the transepts. Almost certainly the Normans added aisles to what had been an aisleless nave, and there is evidence that Norman choir aisles were added in the late twelfth century. In the fourteenth century a new church was built abutting the west end of the abbey church; this church of All Hallows was built for the townsfolk and demolished in 1540.

The abbey church was rebuilt in Perpendicular style in the mid-fifteenth century. The nave arcading is unusual and is probably a Perpendicular rebuilding of the earlier Norman work; this would account for the great thickness of the pillars, caused by panelling being added to a Romanesque core. The nave and choir fan-vaulting are the triumph of the building and in the nave the vault is supported by neither pinnacles nor flying buttresses. There is an intricate pattern of ribs with carved bosses where they cross. The rebus of Abbot Ramsom (which includes a ram within its imagery), who rebuilt the abbey during the Perpendicular period, is prominent in the nave. The design of the vaulting in the choir is even more daring, with transverse ribs that are almost flat; in the mid-nineteenth century flying buttresses were added to protect the roof from collapse. The west front includes Saxon, Norman and Perpendicular work, as does the central tower. The new west window by John Hayward, with the Madonna as its central focus, is a triumph.

The abbey from the south-west

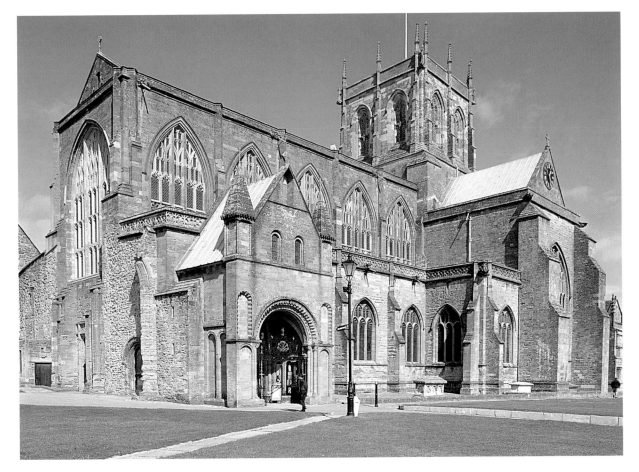

WIMBORNE MINSTER

THE ORIGIN OF Wimborne Minster lies in a Saxon monastery founded by Cuthburga in AD 705. Later a Benedictine abbey church probably occupied the same site as the present minster. King Alfred the Great buried his brother in the minster in 871 and the Saxon church survived until it was burnt by the Danes in 1013. In 1043 Edward the Confessor established a new foundation of secular canons on the site. None of the collegiate buildings, apart from the church, has survived.

On the outside, the church is dominated by the western and central towers. The central crossing tower dates from the late twelfth century but its foundations probably date back to the earlier Saxon church; Romanesque work is clearly visible on the exterior of the tower. The Perpendicular western tower dates from 1464, and houses a peal of ten bells. Entering the church through the north porch, it is best first to visit to the baptistry, beneath the western tower. Here there is a fascinating fourteenth-century astronomical clock. The arches from the baptistry into the nave are Decorated in style and date from around 1350. The nave is Norman but with the first three arcades in the late pointed Transitional style, while the final arcades on the north and south sides nearer the crossing are Romanesque in style.

The crossing instils an air of Norman nobility, with the arches in plain Romanesque style. The basis of both transepts is also Norman, but each has been extended. The north transept was re-fashioned in 1350 by Dean Brembre in the Decorated style, and the south in 1220

The central tower from the south-east

along with the chancel. The great east window with its three lancets is a beautiful example of Early English work. Wimborne contains two other gems, one of which is the splendid crypt which forms the Lady Chapel and dates from 1340 – the Bankes family of Corfe Castle and Kingston Lacy have their burial vaults here. The other gem is on the south side above the choir vestry; here is a small chained library of 240 books, almost a miniature Hereford. Also interesting are the tombs of Daniel Defoe's two daughters in St George's Chapel on the north side of the chancel.

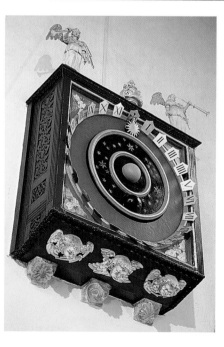

The fourteenth-century astronomical clock

GLASTONBURY ABBEY

SURROUNDING GLASTONBURY ARE legends of Celtic saints, of King Arthur, and of Joseph of Arimathea introduced from the later twelfth century to encourage recruitment and pilgrimage, and to enhance the status of the English Church in Western Europe. However, there was a religious settlement here before a Saxon king added a stone church around 700. Irish scholars taught St Dunstan here in the early tenth century and as abbot of a new community he established the Rule of St Benedict. A fire in 1184 destroyed a magnificent early Norman building.

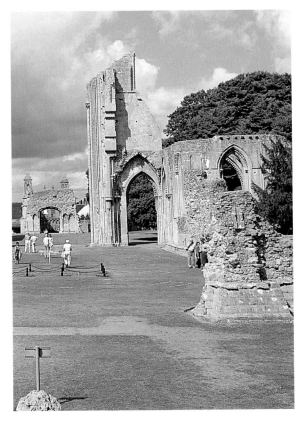

The ruins of Glastonbury Abbey

The new church, beginning at its west end in the fully developed Romanesque style, was not completed until the early sixteenth century. Of the Romanesque work remaining, the Lady Chapel, especially its north door, are very fine. Two of the crossing piers still dominate this evocative ruin; the kitchen of the abbot's house (mid-fourteenth century) has a vaulted lantern roof.

BUCKFAST ABBEY

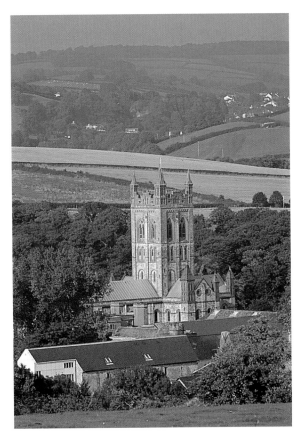

AN ABBEY EXISTED here in Saxon times and as part of a monastic reform movement in the twelfth century, it became a Cistercian monastery, which was then suppressed during the Reformation period in 1539. The buildings gradually fell into a state of disrepair until the nineteenth century, when Buckfast was resettled by Benedictine monks from France. The initiative of Abbot Anscar Vonier, the second abbot of the restored monastery, led to the remarkable rebuilding of the abbey by the monks themselves.

Buckfast Abbey lies in a peaceful valley beside the River Dart

Building began in 1907 and completed in 1937, with the layout conforming exactly to the ground plan of the original monastery. The main walls are of local blue limestone and the window arches, quoins, coping stones and tower turrets are of mellow Ham Hill stone from Somerset. The architectural style is a mixture of Romanesque and early Gothic. Remains of the mediaeval monastery include the Northgate and the undercroft chapel of St Michael (both twelfth century) and, from the fourteenth and fifteenth centuries, the guest hall and Southgate.

EXETER CATHEDRAL

Exeter Cathedral: the west front

WITH THE FLOWERING of Christianity in England in the seventh century through the work of Augustine and Theodore in the South East, and Aidan and Cuthbert in Northumbria, the South West also played a significant part. The most celebrated son of Devonshire at that time was St Boniface. Boniface became a key missionary to central Germany and his shrine can still be visited in the cathedral at Fulda. Willibald records that the young Boniface was educated in a monastery on the site of the present Exeter Cathedral. By petition of Pope Leo IX, Bishop Leofric transferred the see from Crediton to Exeter, and that marked the beginnings of both the diocese and the cathedral as we know it today.

Bishop Leofric, then, pre-empted the move that in most other cathedrals had to await the arrival of the Normans, and moved the see to an important commercial centre. The Normans, however, still left their mark. In 1107, William Warelwast, the nephew

of William the Conqueror, became the bishop of Exeter. Warelwast built the Romanesque cathedral including Exeter's celebrated twin Norman towers which now form the transepts. This arrangement is unique in English cathedrals and is reflected in a similar pattern found in the parish church of Ottery St Mary, near Exeter, which was established by Bishop Grandisson as a foundation for a Vicars' Choral on the model of the cathedral. Bishop Warelwast's cathedral was completed in 1133.

The cathedral as we see it today is the product of a remarkable succession of episcopates, covering, in total, more than one hundred years. The first of these great building bishops was Walter Bronescombe. He arrived in Exeter in 1258. By the time of his death in 1280 the walls of the Lady Chapel reached to the window sills, and the abutting chapels of St Gabriel and St John the Evangelist were almost complete. Bronescombe was succeeded by Bishop Peter Quinel,

*Detail of the carvings in
the Minstrels' Gallery*

whose first achievement was to convert the twin Norman towers into transepts, giving birth to the majestic arches which we still see today. When Quinel died in 1291, the Lady Chapel was finished and he was buried in a tomb which stands before the altar in the Lady Chapel. The third bishop of significance in this work was Bishop Bytton who built the four eastern bays of the choir. The throne, sedilia and the pulpitum screen that divides nave from choir were completed between 1308 and 1326 by Bishop Stapeldon, and the misericords come from this same period. The final bishop of this great quadrumvirate was John Grandisson who was bishop for forty-two years from 1327 to 1369. He built the nave with its thirty Purbeck marble pillars and magnificent Gothic vaulting. There being no central tower, the vaulting continues from one end of the cathedral to the other, forming the longest unbroken stretch of Gothic vaulting in the world. The cathedral remains substantially the building finished by Grandisson. Part of his achievement is the splendid Minstrels' Gallery in the north triforium of the nave which includes superb carvings of minstrels carrying fourteenth-century instruments.

Exeter is notable for its fine tombs and chantry chapels. Amongst these chantries is that founded by Sir John Speke in 1517 – one of the later architectural glories of the cathedral. The Reformation marked the ending of mediaeval patterns of prayer for the dead and the beginning of a different theological approach to death, and the chantry chapels remind us of that older tradition. To the south of the cathedral we can still see some surviving parts of the cloister. Exeter had a cloister even though it is an 'Old Foundation' cathedral whose life was ordered by a dean and canons rather than by a monastic community, as in the case of

Winchester, Worcester and Norwich. Exeter suffered considerably from the ravages of both the Reformation and the Puritan Revolution; images were removed and defaced and the reredos was despoiled – happily this was restored (albeit badly) in 1638. During the Commonwealth a brick wall was built over the screen, effectively producing two churches, one used by the Independents (early Congregationalists) and the other by the Presbyterians. After the Restoration of the Monarchy, the wall was removed and much was done to restore the cathedral's beauty. More recently the cathedral suffered in World War II, with the windows and St James' Chapel particularly badly damaged during aerial bombardment. Exeter Cathedral is now in a splendid state of conservation and it stands as a church of particular and unusual beauty within the South West, reflecting some of the independence of local traditions within this most beautiful part of England.

*The nave looking
towards the great
west window*

TRURO CATHEDRAL

NOWHERE ELSE IN England are the early Celtic roots of Christianity so obvious as with the profusion of local saints in Cornwall. In contrast to this, however, John Loughborough Pearson's Cathedral Church of St Mary the Virgin, in Truro, has the distinction of being the first entirely new foundation since the Reformation. Pearson's vision was of a cathedral in the Anglo-French style tucked into the heart of the city, using the south aisle of the mediaeval parish church of St Mary as the outer south aisle of the new cathedral choir. The whole concept is Gothic revival using a beautifully consistent Early English style. Much of the stone is local – granite from the Mabe for the exterior, and ashlar from St Stephens for the inside of the building, but the finer external detail is in Bath stone.

The nave of eight bays is relatively plain, but as with all of Pearson's churches, it offers distant vistas into other parts of the building – the retro-choir, the transepts and the sanctuary in particular. Both nave and sanctuary have a modest triforium and a high clerestory – the height to the top of the vaulting is 70 feet. The choir and transepts were completed in seven years in 1887. The consecration was performed by Edward White Benson who had moved four years earlier from being the first bishop of Truro to become Archbishop of Canterbury. In the twenty years that followed the nave and central tower, with its spire reaching 250 feet, were completed. The two western towers with their spires were blessed in 1910.

The interior work encompasses some stunning detail. The elaborate and beautiful reredos is of Bath stone with a series of fine sculptures. The baptistry on the south side is a perfect study in Early English with clustered shafts and wall arcading built on shafts of Cornish serpentine. The font and its plinth are of a rose-coloured African marble. The windows of the cathedral form one of the finest collections of English nineteenth- and early-twentieth-century glass. The chapter house is in a modern idiom and was completed and dedicated in 1967. The building's position at the heart of this small Cornish city is unique among English cathedrals and is a powerful focus for the county with its three strong spires.

An aerial view of the cathedral with its three spires reaching up from the heart of the city

GLOSSARY

Words within entries set in **bold** type are themselves defined elsewhere.

aisle in a church, either the areas either side of the **nave**, separated from it by pillars, or a passage running between the rows of seats

ambulatory in a monastery, a **cloister** or place for walking. Often covered and making use of **arcading**

apse a rounded recess with a domed roof, often situated at the end of the **choir**, **aisles** or **nave** of a church

arcading decoration by means of a series of arches

Augustinian of the order of St Augustine of Hippo

aumbry locker or recess in a church wall in which sacramental vessels are stored

baldachino a canopy, usually over an altar or a tomb, supported by columns

barrel vault a vault with a semi-cylindrical roof

baptistry separate building containing the font

basilica a rectangular hall with two rows of columns and an **apse** at the end

Benedictine of the order of St Benedict

boss an ornament fixed at the intersection of the arches which support a **rib vault**

buttress a structure built against a wall to support it, for example a **flying buttress**

Carmelite of the order of Our Lady of Mount Carmel

cellarer the officer of a monastery who was in charge of the cellar

censer a container in which incense is burnt

chancel the part of a church used by clergy and choir, to the east of the **nave** and **transepts**

chantry a small chapel

chapter house a building, often separate, used for meetings of a cathedral or monastic chapter

choir or **quire** that part of a church where the church choir and clergy sit

Cistercian an off-shoot of the Benedictine order, founded at Cîteaux in France in the late eleventh century

clerestory the upper part of a large church, above the level of the roofs of the aisles, where windows let light into the central parts of the church

cloisters covered passages connecting the church to other parts of the monastery

close the enclosed area around a cathedral

Cluniac of the branch of the Benedictine order founded at Cluny in France in the early tenth century

crossing the part of a cathedral where the **nave** intersects with the transept

crypt a subterranean cell, chapel or chamber that is usually vaulted

Curvilinear style of window design of the late **Decorated** period featuring flowing patterns of **tracery**

Decorated architectural period (1307–77) which was characterised by the use of wider windows, projecting **buttresses**, tall pinnacles, and the rapid development of window **tracery** through the **Geometric** and **Curvilinear** styles

dog tooth ornament on **Early English** arches

Dominican of the order of St Dominic

dorter a monastic dormitory

Early English architecture of the earliest phase of the **Gothic** period

fan-vaulting a highly decorative and complex type of vaulting of the later **Gothic** period

feretory a shrine for relics used in procession

flèche a slim spire that rises from point at which the **nave** and **transepts** intersect

flying buttress a prop built out from a pier or other support and supporting the main structure

Franciscan of the order of St Francis of Assisi

front in architecture, any side of a building, usually the one where the entrance is sited

Geometric a style of window design used in the early **Decorated** period centring on geometric shapes used mainly in the fourteenth century. It later developed into the more flowing **Curvilinear** style

Gothic architectural style prevalent in Western Europe from the twelfth to fifteenth centuries. It is characterised by the use of pointed archways

grisaille a particular method of decorative painting on walls or ceilings

hostry equivalent to 'hostelry' and related to 'hospital' and 'hotel', the word basically signifies a place where guests could stay

lancet window high, narrow window with a pointed top

lierne rib vaulting of the **Gothic** period in which the ribs cross each other

locutory part of a monastery set apart for meeting and conversation

misericord a tip-up seat in a church with a projecting shelf on the underside, designed to support those standing at prayer for long periods

narthex a vestibule between the cathedral entrance and the **nave**

nave the main part of a church, running from the main door to the **choir** in a west–east direction

niche a shallow recess in a wall for displaying a statue or other ornament

Perpendicular architectural style (1377–1485), a phase of the **Gothic** period, when the designs of the **Decorated** period developed into longer, taller and more linear forms

pier in architecture, a solid masonry support which sustains vertical pressure

presbytery the part of the church beyond the **choir** at the east end, where only the clergy would enter

pulpitum a large stone or wooden screen or gallery between the **nave** and the **choir**

quatrefoil in architecture, an ornament in the form of a ring of four leaves or petals

quire see **choir**

refectory the dining-room of a monastery

reliquary a small box or shrine for holy relics (the mortal remains of saints)

reredos a decorative screen or painting behind the altar

retable either a shelf for ornaments or a frame for decorative panels, found behind the altar of a church

retro-choir or **retro-quire** the parts of a large church behind the high altar

rib vault a vault built with 'ribs' or arches which support the roof

Romanesque prevalent style of buildings erected in Europe between Roman times and the rise of **Gothic** style in the twelfth century

tracery ornamental stonework in **Gothic** windows

transept the part of a cruciform church which crosses the **nave** in a north–south direction; also each of its two arms (i.e. the north and south **transepts**)

Transitional architecture of the period *c*.1145–*c*.1190, when there was a gradual transition from **Romanesque** to Early **Gothic**

tribune gallery a raised gallery of seats

triforium a gallery or arcade in the wall situated over the arches at the sides of the **nave** and **choir**

turret a small tower which forms part of the structure of a larger building

tympanum the space between door lintel and arch

undercroft a **crypt** or vault below the floor of a church

INDEX